# YOUR
# PRESS RELEASE
## *is*
# BREAKING
### *my*
# HEART

# YOUR
# PRESS RELEASE
*is*
# BREAKING
*my*
# HEART

**A TOTALLY UNCONVENTIONAL GUIDE
TO SELLING *your story* IN THE MEDIA**

*by* JANET MURRAY

*For Katy*
*Forever in my heart*

# ⫸ CONTENTS ⫷

INTRODUCTION **UNBREAK MY HEART** . . . . . . . . . . . . . . . . . . . . . . 1

CHAPTER 1 **SO WHAT EXACTLY IS PR? (AND WHY YOU SHOULD CARE)** . . . . . . . . . . . . . . . . . . . . . 5

CHAPTER 2 **LEAVE YOUR EGO AT THE DOOR: DEVELOPING A PR STRATEGY THAT ACTUALLY WORKS** . . . 11

CHAPTER 3 **HOW MEDIA CONTENT IS CREATED (AND WHY YOU NEED TO KNOW)**. . . . . . . . . . . . . . . . . . 17

CHAPTER 4 **WHY YOU ACTUALLY NEED TO READ OR WATCH THE PROGRAMMES AND PUBLICATIONS YOU'RE PITCHING TO (PLUS SOME NINJA TIPS FOR DOING IT QUICKLY)** . . . . . . . . . . . . . . . . . . 23

CHAPTER 5 **START WITH THE LOW-HANGING FRUIT: GETTING MEDIA COVERAGE WITHOUT PITCHING JOURNALISTS** . . . . . . . . . . . . . . . 29

CHAPTER 6 **NEWSJACKING (FINDING FRESH ANGLES ON HOT NEWS STORIES)** . . . . . . . . . . . . . . . 37

CHAPTER 7 **TELLING MEDIA STORIES PEOPLE ACTUALLY WANT TO HEAR** . . . . . . . . . . . . . . . . . . . . . 47

CHAPTER 8 **HOW TO FIND JOURNALISTS' CONTACT DETAILS (WITHOUT LOOKING LIKE A CRAZY STALKER)** . . . . . . . . . . . . . . . . . . . . 59

CHAPTER 9      **HOW TO WRITE AN AWESOME PITCH OR PRESS RELEASE** . . . . . . . . . . . . . . . . . . . . . **65**

CHAPTER 10      **WHERE (AND WHEN) TO SEND YOUR PITCH OR PRESS RELEASE** . . . . . . . . . . . . . . . . . . . . . **79**

CHAPTER 11      **SOULFUL WRITING: HOW TO WRITE COPY PEOPLE ACTUALLY WANT TO READ** . . . . . . . **85**

CHAPTER 12      **HOW TO 'PR' A PRODUCT LAUNCH** . . . . . . . . **93**

CHAPTER 13      **LANDING A COLUMN IN A NEWSPAPER OR MAGAZINE** . . . . . . . . . . . . . . . . . . . . . . . **103**

CHAPTER 14      **HOW TO SOUND GREAT ON AIR: MEDIA INTERVIEW SKILLS** . . . . . . . . . . . . . . . **107**

CHAPTER 15      **WHY GUEST CONTENT SHOULD BE PART OF YOUR PR STRATEGY** . . . . . . . . . . . . . . . . . . . **115**

CHAPTER 16      **HATERS GONNA HATE: DEALING WITH BEING IN THE MEDIA SPOTLIGHT** . . . . . . . . . . . . . . . **127**

CHAPTER 17      **HIRING A DECENT PR PRO** . . . . . . . . . . . . . . **133**

# ⫸ FOREWORD ⫷

"I have an exciting new product that I'd love to tell you about," are the words that most fill my heart with dread. In my 12 years as a journalist, six of them with a national newspaper and the last three as the editor of the Guardian's Women in Leadership section, I've learnt how to spot an email I don't want to read within the first five words.

Each day I get between 150 and 300 unsolicited emails, each of them containing a pitch or press release that the sender is desperately hoping will grab my attention and result in them being featured. The reality is that most of these will get, at best, a cursory glance before I hit delete and send them to the trash can.

It might have taken you hours to write it, but it's taken me seconds to know it's not right.

You might think your email is unique but believe me, there really is no such thing as a new idea and I have almost definitely seen yours before. What is unique is your story, what made you the person you are and how you came to be where you are today. Not the story that contains clichés like "succeeded as a woman in a male-dominated industry" or "made it against all odds" but the story that you only tell after a few glasses of wine, and when pressed into it by your best friend. That's the story I want to hear – but nobody puts that in a press release.

I first met Janet Murray at the Guardian, when she was working on another section but made a point of coming up and introducing herself. Then a few months later, we met at a networking event and she started to tell me about her work, about how she wanted to help small business owners achieve more media coverage and actually understand what journalists were looking for.

She also told me about what it had been like starting her own business. What had worked and what had failed. What she was excited about, and the bits that absolutely terrified her. She was honest and open and memorable; not only was she teaching businesses exactly how to pitch journalists in a way that would engage them, she was living her values and doing it herself.

When she sent me a pitch a few weeks later, I took the time to read it properly. Rather than trying to pitch her business or tell me the story she wanted me to write in the press, she'd studied my section, thought about who my readers were and had created a pitch that was entirely right for them. The article came in on time, exactly to brief and to date is still one of the most read pieces in the section. Did it bang the drum about her own business? No. Did it get a huge readership and through that send business her way? Yes. Finally here was someone who understood that a good pitch shouldn't be about promoting yourself – it should be about helping journalists create stories their readers want to hear.

Every day, brave entrepreneurs are taking a leap into the unknown and setting up businesses that change peoples' lives. But they're not getting the recognition they deserve and need because they simply don't know how to pitch themselves to the media. Instead they create boring press releases that are ignored by journalists who then miss out on a great story. It's a lose-lose.

What we need is a PR revolution. We need to reject conventional approaches to public relations and get journalists and business owners working together to create stories that really touch the hearts and minds of people who read them. Stories with soul. That's exactly what Janet Murray does and thank God she's finally written a book about it.

*Harriet Minter, Women in Leadership editor, the Guardian*
*July 2016*

# ⫸ INTRODUCTION ⫷

# UNBREAK MY HEART

When I started working as a journalist, 15 years ago, I noticed something pretty early on: people were terrible at selling stories into the media.

I got hundreds of press releases every single day, but most were completely irrelevant to me. What's more, most of the senders had clearly never read any of the publications I wrote for. Yet they'd call me 20 times a day, asking if I'd got their press releases.

After a while, it started to make me feel cross. How could the PR industry be getting it so wrong?

What really galled me was that people were paying for these dreadful press releases. And some of those were small business owners, like me, who were handing over their hard-won cash for this service.

As a freelance journalist – who'd pitched and successfully placed hundreds of articles in the media – I knew exactly how to get an editor interested in a story.

So I started teaching others how to do the same, starting with small workshops in tiny seminar rooms at the YMCA in London, before moving on to large conference style events and, more recently, online training with students from all over the world.

Fifteen years on, I've taught hundreds of people how to sell stories into the media – without hiring a PR company or sending a single press release – and I've written this book so you can do the same.

I'm not saying you should never hire a PR company – or that there aren't good people in the industry – because there are. I just want you to know enough about the media, and how journalists work, so you can make informed decisions about your PR.

Before you read any further, I want you to promise me this: you won't hire a PR company or pay someone to write you a press release before you've got to the end of this book.

Pinky promise?
Good. Let's get started.

PR IS ABOUT
RAISING
*awareness*
*of* WHO YOU ARE,
WHAT YOU DO
*and what*
YOU
STAND FOR

# ⹀CHAPTER 1⹀

# SO WHAT EXACTLY IS PR?
## (AND WHY SHOULD YOU CARE)

I f you're reading this book, I'm guessing you're keen to get media coverage for your business or brand. Perhaps you've tried suggesting ideas to journalists but they've been rejected or ignored. It could be that you've had some success, but would love to get more consistent media coverage.

Or maybe you're so confused about how it all works (do you need to write a press release, how do you find the right journalist to send your idea to, should you call or email, for example) you haven't tried at all.

Whatever your circumstances, what you're doing isn't working as well as you'd like. And you'd love some easy-to-follow guidance that will help you get high-profile media coverage.

I've spent the last 15 years writing and editing for national titles like the Guardian, Daily Telegraph, The Times, BBC Online, Huffington Post, Entrepreneur (to name just a few). In that time, I've commissioned and edited hundreds of articles (and written many more) and made dozens of radio and TV appearances. So I know a thing or two about what journalists are looking for in a media story (and, crucially, what they're not).

In this book, I'm going to walk you through *exactly* what you need to do to get great PR for your business or brand. Follow the steps I lay out for you and you'll get press coverage that will have a positive impact on your business or brand. But if you miss steps out – particularly the research –

then you won't get any at all. And I know I probably sound like your mum....but I don't want to have to say 'I told you so!'

So are you ready to make this PR thing happen? Let's get started...

# WHAT EXACTLY IS PR?

It took me a few years of coaching people in PR and speaking about it at events, to realise I'd overlooked something important: *most people don't really understand what PR is* – even people who say they want help with it.

So if you're confused about what PR actually is and how it can help your business, please be reassured that you're not alone. The following section will get you up to speed. Even if you're not confused, do read the next section anyway, as I explain my unique take on PR, which underpins everything I talk about in this book.

There are dozens of definitions of PR (which stands for 'public relations' by the way) on the internet, many of which are far more complicated than they need to be.

For me, PR is about raising awareness of who you are, what you do and what you stand for through coverage in newspapers, magazines, online publications, and on radio and TV.

In a wider sense, it's also about your public image – about how you show up in the world. This can include anything from the way you dress, the look and feel of your website to how you answer the phone – all of which can have a big impact on how people see you and, crucially, whether they want to do business with you.

However, for the purpose of this book, I'll mainly be talking about PR in terms of coverage in newspapers, magazines, online publications and on radio and TV.

# HOW PR CAN HELP YOUR BUSINESS OR BRAND

I'm going to level with you straight away: if you're looking for a quick-fix solution – to help you boost sales or find clients, for example – don't bother with PR. Put your resources into marketing or advertising.

While you do hear of the odd article that leads to mass sales, for most business owners, PR is a marathon, not a sprint. A one-off feature in a newspaper or radio interview isn't going to make you millions. But a steady stream of newspaper and magazine articles, and radio and TV appearances, over a number of months (or more realistically years) will help you build credibility, influence and brand awareness.

PR can help you win more clients (or the right kind of clients), get better-paid speaking gigs, sell more products, books or whatever it is you do to make a living. But it will take time.

So if you're serious about getting PR, you'll need to roll up your sleeves and put in the groundwork. As with anything you achieve in your business, success is rarely the result of a one-off action. It comes from a series of actions you repeat, day after day, week after week, until you get so good at it, you can almost do it in your sleep.

So I'm sorry I can't give you one single thing you can do that will get you major media coverage tomorrow. But I can give you tons of strategies that will help you get press coverage for years to come.

## SO WHY BOTHER WITH PR?
## A FEW FIGURES FOR YOU:

**Cost of a full-page advert in a regional newspaper:**
around £2k/$3k (based on rate card price)

**Hiring a PR company £12k/$18k a year**
(based on three days a month at a modest rate)

**Cost of a full page advert in a national newspaper**
£20k/$30k (based on rate card price)

**Cost of getting coverage in a magazine or newspaper £0/$0**

It gets better; not only is coverage in the media absolutely free, it's also better for your business or brand. A journalist choosing to feature you because they think their audience will be interested in what you do (rather than because you've thrown a wad of cash at them for an advert) will give you far more credibility.

## SO WHY NOT HIRE A PR SPECIALIST?

If you're short on time, it's tempting to think hiring a PR company is some kind of magic bullet. You pay experts to come up with story ideas, write press releases and contact journalists – while you get on with with running your business.

In practice, it doesn't generally work like that. No PR company/consultant will know your business or organisation like you do. So you'll still need to spend time – quite a bit at first – briefing them about it. And you probably won't want to put them in direct contact with journalists until you're sure they know *exactly* what you're about.

Even when they're up to speed, you still have a problem: *most journalists don't like dealing with PR companies.*

If you're reading this, and run or work for a PR company I know you won't like hearing this. But from a journalist's point of view, PR people can be annoying. They can't always answer all your questions, they have to liaise with their clients to arrange interviews and they generally act as a barrier to the people you want to talk to. Ultimately, they slow things down, which is frustrating for journalists, who are usually working to tight deadlines.

That aside, there is some pretty bad practice out there. While I know first-hand that there are some brilliant PR professionals, I've come across many more who have never spent any time in a newsroom and – there's no nice way of putting this – wouldn't know a good story if it hit them in the face. They're writing pointless press releases, creating press kits or case studies (and other resources you don't actually need), giving silly advice – and charging a lot of money for it. This means that the good PRs (and if you're reading this, I just *know* you're one of the good ones) can often find it more difficult to get journalists' attention. Totally unfair, I know – but that's how it is – and I'm a big believer in working with what you've got rather than how you'd like things to be.

If you do run or work for a PR company and have picked up this book *please don't put it down.* Not only am I going to teach you strategies that will make your job easier, I'm also going to share some ideas that will help you deal with journalists (even the ones who don't like PRs). So even if you hate me right now, I reckon you might hate me a little bit less by the end of this book. In fact, you might even like me.

## YOU CAN TOTALLY DO THIS

This stuff isn't rocket science; anyone with a great idea, and a bit of common sense can pitch a story into the media. And if you're willing to invest just a few hours a week in researching the publications and programmes you'd like to be featured in, you can generate your own PR opportunities. In fact, if you're doing it right, getting press coverage can be as easy as firing off a quick email or making a few phone calls.

I'm not saying you should never outsource your PR, but I do think all small business owners should have some hands-on involvement – at least at first. After all, if you have no idea how to get an article in the newspaper or get yourself on the radio, how can you tell if your PR company is providing value for money?

## WHAT TO EXPECT

If you're new to PR – or looking to up your game – prepare for a bumpy ride. PR isn't rocket science, but understanding the media (and how journalists think) does take time and a bit of trial and error.

As you start applying the principles in this book, I can pretty much guarantee that your ideas will get rejected and/or ignored at some point. You may find yourself hearing the word 'no' more than 'yes' at first. Or you may have a couple of initial successes, then hit a plateau. This may leave you feeling hurt, frustrated, annoyed, embarrassed...and a whole host of other emotions, but please feel reassured that this is all completely normal. If you're consistent, persistent and willing to learn from your mistakes, you will get there in the end. Guaranteed.

# WHAT DO JOURNALISTS *want?*

## GREAT CONTENT THAT IS A PERFECT FIT *for their* AUDIENCE

# CHAPTER 2

# LEAVE YOUR EGO AT THE DOOR

## DEVELOPING A PR STRATEGY THAT ACTUALLY WORKS

A few years back, we moved into an old property that needed new windows. We invited two companies round to give us a quote for replacing them.

The first – let's call him Window Salesman 1 – arrived at 7pm and spent three hours showing us endless samples and talking about the way his windows were made, before giving us a price – which he said he could only guarantee if we signed up there and then. When we said we needed time to discuss his quotation between ourselves, he tried to persuade us to change our minds. Seeing we weren't going to budge, his tactics got more and more desperate. 'You know I could sell you these windows if I wanted to...' he whimpered, as I showed him the door.

The following day, we had a visit from a rival company. Having lost a whole evening to Window Salesman 1, we were dreading it. But Window Salesman 2 simply measured our windows, gave us a price for what we wanted and answered our questions – like who would fit the windows, how long it would take and how long we'd have to wait for installation. He was gone within 30 minutes.

Guess which company got our business?

Company 2 was actually a little more expensive but we chose them because they *gave us exactly what we needed.* It was great customer service, not sales tactics that made us buy those windows.

In 15 years as a national journalist and editor, I've come across a lot of people who remind me of Window Salesman 1. People who think getting journalists' attention is about quantity (i.e. how many press releases you send or phone calls you make) rather than quality. People who make absolute pests of themselves: sending the same press release six times, calling up endlessly to see if you've got their email and arguing with your decision when you say 'no' to them. Like Window Salesperson 1 they have an air of desperation about them which is not only really unattractive, it also means journalists generally show them the door.

If you want to get media coverage for your business or brand, you need to serve journalists. That's not about being a suck up; it's about making it as easy as possible for journalists to do business with you – making sure you're available when you say you are, delivering on your promises and the little added extras (like offering good-quality photographs, without even being asked).

It's also about putting journalists' needs before your own.

Now you might be thinking 'hang on a minute, how can putting journalists' needs before my own help me get media coverage?' Well, here's the thing: PR isn't about persuasion. It doesn't matter how many press releases you send or phone calls you make, if your story isn't interesting, journalists aren't going to run it. The only way to get media coverage is to offer journalists great content that is a perfect fit for their audience. And I'm going to show you exactly how to do just that.

## CREATING YOUR MEDIA VISION

Press coverage may be free, but your time isn't, so the more strategic you can be with your PR the better. You may need to kick your ego in the shins though; while you may love the idea of being featured in Vogue or on CNN, if the people you want to get in front of read the Wall Street Journal or some obscure industry title barely anyone's heard of, that's where you need to be.

GET CURIOUS *about* HOW MEDIA CONTENT IS *put* TOGETHER

So before you even attempt to get press coverage for your business or brand, you need to ask yourself the following questions:

*Why am I doing this?*

It doesn't really matter what your objective is (it could be anything from getting more clients to more high profile speaking gigs) – what's important is that you have one. Having a clear objective will help you decide which publications and programmes you should be targeting and what kind of content might work for them.

You may have more than one objective; perhaps you want to get more clients, secure more high-profile gigs *and* build your reputation in a partic-ular industry. That's absolutely fine (and completely normal) but if you don't want to feel overwhelmed, you'll need to prioritise. I'd suggest focus-ing on one objective for a fixed period of time (e.g. 30 days) before moving on to the next.

You may also find your objectives change over time. That's fine too – so long as you keep checking in with your PR activities to make sure they align with your overall business objectives.

*Who do I need to get in front of to make that happen?*

Once you're clear on your objective, think about who you need to get in front of to make it happen. The more specific you can be the better. For exam-ple, 'parents' is a pretty broad audience. 'Parents of twins or multiples' or 'parents with children with speech and language difficulties' is much more precise and will help you pinpoint the kind of publications and pro-grammes (and the specific sections within them) you should be targeting.

*Find out what they read, watch and listen to*

Once you're clear on who you need to get in front of, find out what they read, watch and listen to. This will help you decide which publications and programmes to target.

If you're wondering how to find out...just ask. Creating an online survey or questionnaire using an online tool like Survey Monkey or Wufoo takes minutes and a small sample (between 10 and 50 is ideal) of people who fit your target audience can provide you with enough information to create a shortlist.

*Make a shortlist of target publications*

Next, make a list of the publications or programmes you'd like coverage in. If you're new to PR – or working with a new client – I'd suggest starting small. Limiting your shortlist to three to five publications will feel less overwhelming and, once you've conquered those, you can always add more.

## OVER TO YOU

Set aside half an hour to work through the questions in this chapter and create your media vision. Head over to www.janetmurray.co.uk/books to download your media vision worksheet.

## USEFUL LINKS

Survey Monkey: *www.surveymonkey.co.uk*
Wufoo: *www.wufoo.com*

# ≡ CHAPTER 3 ≡

# HOW MEDIA CONTENT
# IS CREATED

## (AND WHY YOU NEED TO KNOW)

I magine turning up to a job interview without researching the company, stalking your interviewer(s) on LinkedIn or thinking about the questions you might be asked (and preparing your answers).

It's pretty unlikely you'd get the job, isn't it?

Yet this is, essentially, what people do to journalists, every day of the week.

They send pitches and press releases without actually reading the publication or watching/listening to the programme. As if this isn't insulting enough, they send *exactly the same* pitch or press release to journalists on different publications or programmes.

The message is this: *"I want you to help me, by giving me column inches or airtime, but I'm not prepared to put in the time to understand exactly what you need."*

Then they wonder why they get turned down – or completely ignored – by journalists.

If you want to give yourself the best possible chance of getting coverage in a magazine or newspaper (or on radio or TV), you must spend time researching the publications/programmes you're pitching so you can get a sense of the kind of content they typically run.

While it's tempting to take the easy option (firing a press release off to a bunch of journalists and crossing your fingers someone will pick it up) this is a pretty ineffective way of doing PR. To increase your chances of media coverage, you need to send a tailored pitch (and by 'pitch' I mean an email that sells your idea) to every single publication or programme you approach.

In this chapter, I'm going to show you the right way to research publications and programmes so you'll know exactly what to put in every pitch you send. It may take you a little bit of time at first, but once you've got the hang of it, you'll be able to look at any publication or programme and identify the opportunities to get media coverage – in a matter of minutes.

But, first off, a bit of essential background information.

## UNDERSTANDING MEDIA CONTENT

The recent explosion in online content means understanding how the media works has never been so complicated. With more people producing more content across more platforms in more formats e.g. video, audio, text and images, it can feel really confusing. But the more you understand about the media – and how journalists work – the better equipped you'll be to deliver your message in the media.

In today's complicated media landscape, there are five main types of media content.

These are:

1. **Social media.** May be created or curated by anyone who has access to social media platforms and may take the form of text, video, audio or visual content.

2. **Single-author blogs/podcasts.** These are typically run by an individual who produces most of the content, but may feature guest contributors. While some single-author blogs or podcasts have an information page (or even a dedicated contact form) for prospective contributors, many others don't, so if you want to contribute to the site, you'll probably need to contact the owner direct.

3. **Multi-author blogs e.g. Mind Body Green or Tiny Buddha.** May be run by an individual or a small team, but the content is produced by multiple authors. Multi-author blogs generally feature an information page or dedicated contact form for prospective contributors, along with an email address to send content to (usually the completed article rather than a pitch – but do check first).

4. **Large media sites e.g. Huffington Post or Entrepreneur** These are run more along the lines of the traditional media (i.e. newspapers and magazines) and have a core editorial team of journalists who create content and commission guest articles from multiple authors.

   While large media sites often have an information page or dedicated contact form for prospective contributors, along with a generic email address to send content to (usually the completed article rather than a pitch – but do check first), building relationships with specific editors can be a better route in.

5. **Traditional or mainstream media e.g. Guardian, New York Times, Sydney Morning Herald.** Most people assume that mainstream media has the biggest impact on your business and brand, but this isn't always the case. While you do hear of the odd article that goes viral, most people need a steady stream of newspaper and magazine articles and radio & TV appearances, over a number of months to start building brand awareness in the mainstream media.

Sharing content on social media, blogs and large media sites doesn't always carry the same kudos as traditional media, but it can deliver a quicker return on investment and measurable results (an increase in web traffic, social media followers and/or sales, for example).

While there is great value in creating other kinds of content, in this book, I'm going to focus on the last two – large media sites and traditional or mainstream media.

# HOW PUBLICATIONS AND PROGRAMMES ARE PUT TOGETHER

If you don't work on a magazine or newspaper, it's easy to assume they're put together in a rather 'ad hoc' way i.e. when the editor starts putting together a new issue, they sit down with a blank piece of paper and think 'hmmm....what should I include this time round?'

In fact, publications and programmes (and this goes for radio and TV too) have quite a rigid structure. For example, if you look at a daily newspaper, over a week, you'll probably notice these sorts of things:

- The news stories are in the same place and take up a similar number of pages in every issue

- The features (longer stories that look at issues in more depth) also take up a similar number of pages in each issue even though the content might be different (for example, many newspapers' features sections have a focus for each day e.g. health, technology, the arts, lifestyle)

- There are a number of opinion articles each day (there may even be a specific section for this) some of which are written by regular column-ists, others by guest experts

- There may be other types of content e.g. an interview with a famous person, a Q & A with a business owner or a first-person style confes-sional. As with the other types of content you'll probably notice they pop up on the same (or similar) page in every issue

Although it can be more challenging to decode, you'll also see the same pat-terns on online publications and radio and TV i.e. regular 'slots' that are filled with similar content. If you take a quick skim through an online publication like Fast Company, for example, you'll see their content comes under different themes (often referred to as 'verticals') e.g. 'hit the ground running' (advice and inspiration for new businesses) or 'your most productive self' (productivity hacks). The Huffington Post also has 'verticals' e.g. family, health and fitness, politics and studying the ones that relate to your area of expertise should give you an idea of the kinds of topics that work well for its audience.

On radio or TV news programmes you will also notice patterns. For example, the breakfast show on my local radio covers two big news stories an hour plus a lighter one. The news is on the hour, half hour and quarter of an hour and there is also a newspaper review (led by a guest in the studio) at around 25 minutes past the hour.

When you start getting curious about how programmes and publications are put together, you'll soon see that there is nothing random about the way media content is planned. And the more you understand about how different publications and programmes are put together – and the kind of content they typically run – the better chance you'll have of success. So you won't make the mistake of offering an interview to a publication that never runs interviews or an article on dealing with toddler tantrums to a women's magazine that doesn't cover parenting. You'll also get a sense of how much content they run each day (or week or month) and who creates it (i.e. whether it's staff journalists, freelance writers or business owners/leaders).

## OVER TO YOU

Set aside a couple of hours to go to a big bookshop that sells magazines or newspapers – preferably one that stocks everything from national newspapers to niche industry titles. Scour the shelves for the kind of publications you think are read by your target audiences, grab a coffee and spend some time looking at them. You'll need to do some online research too, but if you really want to understand how publications are put together, as a reporter friend of mine puts it so charmingly...you need to get your fingers grubby.

## USEFUL LINKS

Mind Body Green: *www.mindbodygreen.com*
Tiny Buddha: *tinybuddha.com*
Huffington Post: *www.huffingtonpost.com*
Entrepreneur: *www.entrepreneur.com*
Fast Company: *www.fastcompany.com*

THE BETTER YOU
KNOW THE
*publications &*
*programmes*
YOU'RE PITCHING TO,
THE GREATER
YOUR CHANCES OF
SUCCESS

# ⧦ CHAPTER 4 ⧦

# WHY YOU ACTUALLY NEED TO READ OR WATCH THE PROGRAMMES AND PUBLICATIONS YOU'RE PITCHING TO
## (PLUS SOME NINJA TIPS FOR DOING IT QUICKLY)

**W**hen I'm working as a commissioning editor on a newspaper, I get several emails a day that say something like this:

"I run my own online diet club. Would you be interested in writing about it?"

Not only is this incredibly vague, the underlying message is this: *I want you to give me space in your publication but I want you to do all the work figuring out how to tackle the story.'*

Most journalists get hundreds of pitches and press releases each week, so if you send something like this, they'll probably just ignore you.

The more specific you can be about the kind of story you're pitching to a journalist – and where it might appear in the publication – the more successful you're likely to be.

For example: *'I'd like to write something for your 'Food Police' section on why most diets don't work'* is much better than saying 'Would you be interested in writing about my online diet club?'

In order to be this specific, you do need to know the publication or programme you're pitching to inside out. You also need to understand the different *types* of media content e.g. news stories, features, opinion articles it generally runs, so you can tailor your offering.

This will also help you get your head round another key question (something people ask me about all the time) – whether you'll have to write the article yourself or whether a journalist will write it.

Here's a quick summary of the different kinds of media content you'll find in print publications (plus a few tips for radio and TV). Do be aware, however, that there are always exceptions.

A **news story** is a short, factual article (often around 300-500 words) that is written in the third person and informs you of the latest developments in a story. In a print publication, the news section is usually at or near the front. On TV or radio, news stories are often broadcast on the hour or half hour, in a bulletin. If you pitch a news story, a journalist will generally write it.

An **investigative feature** is a longer article (generally 800 words or above) that explores a topic in-depth. A feature may open with a quotation or a piece of descriptive writing and, although often written in the third person, it will feel less 'immediate' than a news story, delving much more into the past and maybe even gazing into the future. On TV and radio, features are generally longer and more in-depth than news stories.

If you pitch a feature, a journalist will generally write it. But do be aware that there are different kinds of features, including the so-called 'stunt feature' where you try something out (this could be anything from one-armed juggling to not judging people for a week) and share your experience. It goes without saying you'll be asked to write this kind of feature – who else could?

An **interview** is often written in the third person and is similar in length to a feature. However, some publications use a Q & A style or 'first person' style interviews. If you pitch an interview, a journalist will probably write it, but you could be asked to submit answers to questions via email.

A **review** is another type of feature, which is usually written in the third person and is – as the name suggests – a 'review' of a book, product or service. If you suggest something for a review – a round-up of the best beach bags, Mother's Day presents or gadgets under £20, for example – a journalist will generally write it.

An **opinion article** is written in the first person and expresses an point of view. Word lengths can vary, but 600-800 words is about average. To give you a few examples, I've written opinion articles on why I don't like holidays (Huffington Post), why women should stop working for free (Guardian) and why exams are getting easier (New Statesman). If you pitch this kind of article, you will be asked to write it (or at least provide the words).

A **first-person or 'confessional'** article is an account of something that has happened to you – often something that has influenced your life in a profound way. To give you a few examples, I've written first person articles on being diagnosed with a serious liver disorder, not being able to have any more children and why I sent my child to a fee-paying school (a bit of context – this is quite a divisive issue in the UK).

If you pitch this kind of story, you will usually be asked to write it (or at least provide the words), although there are some exceptions – for example first-person style interviews, where the journalist will interview you and write it up.

A **'how to'** feature is a practical article, where you teach people a concept or skill they can apply in their life or work. If you pitch this kind of story, you will almost certainly be asked to write it (or at least provide the words).

To give you a few examples, I've written 'how to' articles on everything from how to write a press release (Guardian), find the ideal university course for your child (Times) to how entrepreneurs can get PR (Entrepreneur).

If you're a small business owner – unless you have a really unusual product or service – you're far more likely to be able to place stories that fall into the last three categories.

# HOW TO RESEARCH YOUR TARGET PUBLICATIONS

I often hear journalists complaining that most people who pitch to them haven't even looked at their publication or programme...which is why their ideas are so off-piste. In my experience, this isn't strictly true; most people do attempt to research the publications or programmes they're pitching to...they just don't do it in the right way.

When I talk about research, I don't mean a cursory flick through a magazine, a five minute tour of a website or a quick listen to a radio show while you're doing something else.

I mean studying your target publications/programmes like you were swotting up for an exam: setting aside time, with no other distractions, to do the following (ideally across at least three back editions or episodes).

**Create a 'flatplan' of the publication.** This is the tool journalists use to plan the content of a magazine or newspaper and is – just as the name suggests – a flat (i.e. 2D) plan of the publication where you can see every page. Go through a publication you'd like to get coverage in and write down what you see on every page (including the adverts) and you'll soon get a feel for the types of content e.g. news, features, opinion articles it typically runs.

**Make lists of the kinds of articles or items they generally run**, paying particular attention to the headlines and any that relate to your specific area of expertise. You'll need about 15-20 headlines to get a good sense of how the publication or programme works.

**Note down the names of any regular slots** e.g. interviews, opinion articles and who writes them (are they written by in-house journalists, regular contributors or does it look like they commission content from other sources? If they do, it could be a great opportunity for you to get some media coverage).

**Note down the names (and contact details)** of their journalists and editors (there's more on how to find them in Chapter 8) and start following them. This will help you get a better sense of what kind of content might work for them.

# OVER TO YOU

Head over to www.janetmurray.co.uk/books, grab some of my flatplan blanks and a publication you'd like to get featured in. Go through it and write down *exactly* what you see on each page This should quickly give you a sense of the structure of the publication, the balance of different content (i.e. news, features, opinion) and the kind of content they generally run. I'd recommend you 'flatplan' every publication you want to get coverage in (it can be a big lightbulb moment when you're struggling to work out what might be of interest to an editor) but start with one and see what you discover – otherwise you could end up feeling overwhelmed.

# START
*by*
*connecting*
*with*
## JOURNALISTS
### WHO ARE LOOKING
### FOR HELP WITH
# STORIES

# CHAPTER 5

# START WITH THE LOW-HANGING FRUIT

## GETTING MEDIA COVERAGE WITHOUT PITCHING JOURNALISTS

When I first started teaching PR, I used to throw people in at the deep end. I'd have them developing story ideas, writing pitches and emailing journalists – right from the off. But while some relished the challenge, others went into overwhelm. They'd get so paralysed by fear, they'd end up doing nothing at all.

The more people I worked with, the more I realised that, while PR isn't rocket science, there are quite a few 'moving parts'. I now encourage people to start with the lowest-hanging fruit. No pitching. No writing press releases. Just responding to journalists who are already looking for help. Not only does this get you used to dealing with journalists – exchanging emails, following their brief and giving interviews, for example – it can also help you get a better sense of what they're looking for and how they work. Once you're comfortable with that, you can move into pitching mode.

With that in mind, here are some things you can do to get press coverage – without the stress of writing pitches and press releases.

If you've got some experience of PR, please don't skip this section, as I can pretty much guarantee you're not doing some of the things I suggest that could be 'easy wins' for you.

## HOW TO CONNECT WITH JOURNALISTS WHO ARE ALREADY LOOKING FOR HELP WITH STORIES

There are three main ways you can connect with journalists who are looking for help with stories. These are:

1. Responding directly to their requests on social media

2. Using media enquiry services

3. Making yourself more easily 'found' online

There are two main ways you can respond to journalists who are actively looking for people to talk to – using Twitter hashtags like #journorequest or via media enquiry services like Response Source, Journolink or Help A Reporter Out which connect journalists with people who want to be featured in the media.

Type the #journorequest or #prrequest hashtag into the Twitter search box and you'll find dozens of requests from journalists and bloggers looking for help with specific articles or programmes. To give you a few examples, I just put the #journorequest hashtag into Twitter and found requests about pricing for small business owners, the best personal budgeting apps and people who've had skin cancer diagnosed by their GP – all of which I could help with.

The last involves a family member but, providing they're willing to be involved, it's still worth following up. Offering to help journalists out on stories that won't necessarily get you a mention for your business or brand can be a good move, as it's moving you from 'stranger' to 'friend' status.

As the sales expert Matthew Kimberley pointed out when I interviewed him for my podcast recently, "it's much easier to say no to strangers." Doing a journalist a favour – even when there's nothing in it for you – makes you memorable. It also means that when you do have a story to pitch, they're far more likely to read your email or take your call.

This is still worth doing, even if the journalist involved doesn't work on any of your target publications. Not only do journalists move around a lot (that junior reporter on a niche industry publication may end up on the glossy consumer magazine you'd love to be featured in some day), they also tend to have friends who work on other publications or programmes, who are also looking for help with stories.

So by doing this one simple thing, every day – reading and responding to journalists' requests on Twitter – you're building your network of media contacts. That's a pretty powerful thing.

And don't just focus on Twitter. While there are fewer journalists looking for people to talk to on social media sites like Instagram and Facebook, it can be easier to stand out in a less crowded space.

A few last words on hashtags: the two I've mentioned are mainly used in the UK, but a quick Twitter search should throw up PR hashtags that are commonly used in your part of the world.

It's also worth pointing out that following journalist request hashtags can be a great way to see how journalists find new angles on current media stories (a strategy known as 'newsjacking' that I'll teach you in Chapter 6). For example, in the search I've just done, I noticed quite a few requests about plus-size women. I'm pretty sure this is because there is a big media story doing the rounds at the moment about Facebook turning down an ad featuring a plus-size woman.

## USING MEDIA ENQUIRY SERVICES

Sign up to a media enquiry service like Response Source, Help A Reporter Out, Gorkana, Journolink or Sourcebottle and you'll get regular email updates from journalists who are looking for experts and case studies to feature in their work. Some are free and others offer free trials, so you can start building your media contact database immediately.

# MAKING YOURSELF MORE EASILY FOUND ONLINE

Journalists are always looking for experts to comment on stories they're covering. And the first thing they do when a story breaks – particularly if it's a subject they're not familiar with – is a Google search.

Having up-to-date social media profiles (with a 24/7 contact number), posting regular content that shows your expertise (rather than telling people about it) and, ideally – having your own blog will make you much more visible to journalists.

With that in mind, here's a quick rundown of how you can use social media to make it easier for journalists to find you.

# TWITTER

Twitter is where most journalists hang out, so making Twitter lists of journalists you're keen to connect with can be a smart move. Checking in daily to see what they're talking about will not only help you get an idea of the topics they're particularly interested in, you might also spot them asking for help with stories they're working on.

Once you've found a journalist you want to connect with on Twitter, start building relationships by sharing and commenting on their posts. That way, when you pop up in their inbox with a story idea, they should recognise your name. Don't overdo it though – there's a fine line between looking interested and stalking.

It's worth bearing in mind that many journalists use Twitter like a search engine, particularly when they're looking for people to talk to for stories they're working on. So having an up-to-date profile, sharing content that relates to your area of expertise and using hashtags – which group together posts on a similar topic – can be a good move. If there's anything you're particularly keen to raise awareness of, you might also want to add a pinned post at the top of your feed

If a big story is breaking, journalists may also use geotags (an electronic tag that assigns a geographical tag to a photo or video) to find people to talk to in a particular area – another reason why it's worth being active on Twitter.

There's no reason why you can't suggest an idea to a journalist on Twitter, but do be aware that once your idea is out there, it isn't exclusive anymore, which can be off-putting. Sending a tweet saying you have a story idea and asking if it's ok for you to send a direct message (they'll need to follow you back for you to do that) is usually better.

And don't 'spam' journalists with story ideas on Twitter. If a journalist can see from your feed that you've pitched exactly the same idea to dozens of other journalists, they're unlikely to be interested (particularly if you're sharing it with competing programmes or titles).

# LINKEDIN

Many journalists are listed on LinkedIn, so if you're looking to find the name of a journalist in a particular role on a specific publication or pro-gramme e.g. deputy editor or producer, it can be a useful resource.

Do bear in mind that journalists also look for people to talk to on LinkedIn, so having an up-to-date profile – ideally with examples of your work and/or a short video of clip of you talking or presenting is a good idea. If it's immediately obvious that you know your subject – and are a good talker – journalists are much more likely to want to speak to you.

Take particular care with your 'professional headline' (the one-liner under your name). While it's tempting to put your title e.g. 'Director of leadership coaching company' or 'Employer engagement co-ordinator' this will mean nothing to a busy journalist. Explaining how you help people e.g. 'I help women become CEOs ' or 'I help writers make better decisions about money' and you'll have much more chance of grabbing their attention.

Creating content for LinkedIn Pulse – a platform where users can share their own content – can be another way get to noticed. Not only are posts search-engine-friendly (which means, thanks to the authority of LinkedIn itself, content gets ranked relatively quickly), it also boosts your authority and keeps you front-of-mind with your followers (which is not just useful for attracting journalists – it can also help you attract new business).

There's no reason why you can't message journalists with story ideas on LinkedIn, but I wouldn't hold your breath waiting for a reply. Most seem to use it for job hunting – or to make themselves more easily found by employers – so if you're looking to pitch story ideas, Twitter is probably a better bet.

## FACEBOOK

Posting regular content on your Facebook page that shows your expertise – links to blog posts or talks you've given, for example – can help journalists find you more easily.

On the flip side, do be aware that some journalists trawl Facebook groups – particularly community 'noticeboards' – for potential stories. So always be mindful of what you're sharing – you never know who might be reading.

## INSTAGRAM

Following journalists you're keen to connect with on Instagram can be a great way to connect. Checking in daily to see what they're talking about, will help you get an idea of what topics they're particularly interested in. Get yourself on their radar by liking and sharing their content, but as with Twitter, remember there's a fine line between looking interested and stalking.

Remember, also, that having a great Instagram feed can be newsworthy in itself. For example, the Gaybeards – two friends who post pictures of themselves with their beards 'dressed up' in various ways – got loads of media coverage last Christmas for their Instagram campaign showing photographs of them covering their beards in glitter.

# SNAPCHAT

While there are fewer journalists hanging out on the mobile messaging app Snapchat at the moment, that isn't necessarily a bad thing. In fact it means you'll stand out more. So finding journalists who are hanging out on Snapchat and following them can be a good way to find out more about what they're interested in.

Unlike some of the other social media platforms, it seems to be more socially acceptable to message new connections on Snapchat to say 'hi' – so you don't need to worry so much about being a stalker. Go ahead and introduce yourself.

# PERISCOPE

As with Snapchat, there are fewer journalists hanging out on Twitter's live streaming app Periscope, but there are advantages. Finding journalists who are active on Periscope, watching their 'scopes' and sending messages can be a great way to connect.

If a big story is breaking, journalists may also use geotags to find people to talk to in a particular area – another reason why it's worth being active on Twitter.

# OVER TO YOU

Head over to www.janetmurray.co.uk/books where you can find video tutorials on how to set up Twitter lists and how to use Twitter to connect with journalists. Sign up for trials of media enquiry services and start building your media database.

# USEFUL LINKS

Response Source: *www.responsesource.com*
Gorkana: *www.gorkana.com*
Help A Reporter Out: *www.helpareporter.com*
Sourcebottle: *www.sourcebottle.com*
Journolink: *www.journolink.com*

FIND

A fresh

ANGLE

on a

HOT

NEWS STORY

# ═ CHAPTER 6 ═

# NEWSJACKING

## (FINDING FRESH ANGLES ON HOT NEWS STORIES)

A few weeks ago, I got an email from an editor at the Independent newspaper. A new report had been published which suggested that premature babies were more likely to be unemployed as adults. As my own daughter was born 12 weeks early, the editor (who I happen to know already) wondered if I was interested in writing an opinion article on the topic – specifically on whether research like this stigmatises children.

This is an example of **newsjacking –** finding a fresh angle on a current news story and using it to create another piece of media content e.g. an opinion article, interview or feature. Journalists do it all the time and, the good news is, you can do it too.

Here are a few more examples that will help you understand how newsjacking works.

Let's say you specialise in developing software to manage nuisance calls. You wake up one morning to find the topic is headline news, due to an announcement that the government is planning to introduce harsher penalties for companies who cold call households. So you contact the producers of various radio and TV shows to offer expert comment on the topic. Knowing it's a subject the public will care about, you also pitch an opinion article to a national newspaper on the topic.

Or perhaps you run a popular fashion blog for the over-forties. It's Oscars night and everyone is talking about a big movie star's fashion faux pas. Knowing it will be a hot topic on all the big TV/radio breakfast shows in the morning, you give them all a call and offer expert comment. You also pitch an opinion article to a national newspaper on the subject.

Maybe you read a story about a woman who is spending £1000 on her children for Christmas. You're not buying your children Christmas presents – because you're on a family mission not to buy anything for a year – and you're making presents instead. So you contact the newspaper involved to see if they'd be interested in covering your story.

These are all real examples of clients – or people I know – who have used newsjacking to get media coverage for their business or brand.

But before I get into the nitty gritty of how to to 'newsjack', I need to say this: timing is everything. In a 24/7 news culture, where social media is driving the news agenda at breakneck speed, you need to act fast.

When you pitch an idea to a journalist in the traditional media (e.g. Guardian, New York Times, Sydney Morning Herald), the first thing they'll ask themselves is: *'why do people need to hear about this now?'* (or tomorrow, next week or next month – depending on how far ahead you're pitching). This is generally referred to as a story 'hook' or 'peg'. And while you might have a great story idea, if there isn't an obvious 'hook' for it, journalists probably won't be interested in running it.

So if you wake up in the morning to a breaking news story that relates to your area of expertise, you can't afford to wait until you've had your breakfast, dropped your kids off at school or written your weekly blog post. You need start emailing or calling journalists straight away or you'll miss the opportunity.

# HOW TO NEWSJACK

While newsjacking might seem like a spontaneous activity, there is actually quite a lot you can do to prepare. Understanding how journalists gather stories can help a lot.

When journalists are planning content, they often refer to stories as 'on' and 'off' diary.

'On diary' refers to events you can predict – from obvious things like Christmas, Mother's Day or the summer holiday season to the publication of annual reports or surveys.

These are marked on journalists' diaries months – or even years – in advance. Not only does this ensure they don't miss important stories, it also gives them plenty of time to carry out research and find experts and case studies to talk to.

'Off diary' refers to events you can't necessarily predict – from a celebrity speaking out of turn to terrorist attacks or natural disasters.

If you want to get more media coverage for your business or brand, you need to be pitching both 'on' and 'off diary' stories – and the good news is newsjacking works for both.

If you want more 'on diary' coverage, you need a calendar – ideally one that gives you a month-per-view – where you can mark up any key dates/events, across the year, that could provide 'hooks' for media stories. Personally I think a wall calendar – which you post up somewhere you can see it all the time in your office – can work better than an online tool, but obviously this is up to you.

You'll need to set aside at least a couple of hours to mark up your media calendar (I recommend planning up to 12 months ahead) but I promise you the upfront time investment will be worth it.

Here are the kinds of things you should include:

**The blinkin' obvious stuff** like Christmas, New Year, Easter, Summer, Halloween and so on. This may sound obvious, but when you're busy with other things it's easy to get sidetracked. Say you're a fitness specialist and have some great story ideas around getting the perfect beach body; most consumer magazines work 3-6 months ahead, so leave it until March to pitch it to a journalist and you could find you've left it too late.

**Important political events** like budget days, government spending reviews, elections, party conferences, parliamentary debates, select committee meetings and so on.

If you're a wedding planner or a personal trainer, you might be wondering how political events can help you get press coverage for your business. Think again.

One of the best examples of small business PR I've seen was from wedding and events planner Sarah Poole, who fronted a campaign to urge the UK government to stop closing a busy road leading to the port of Dover when it got too congested. In speaking to national media like the BBC and Daily Telegraph about how this was hurting small business owners, Sarah not only showed she was a passionate entrepreneur, she also put her venue, Westenhanger Castle, on the map.

Whether you're a leadership coach or a hair salon owner you are affected by political issues – from taxation to business law to changes in government policy – and these can all provide great 'hooks' for stories.

**Awareness days** e.g. Cancer awareness day, National Orgasm Week (yes, really!) or Mental Health Awareness Day (more about that later).

**Court cases**. You might also want to add details of court cases that relate to your industry or sector. So let's say you run a restaurant, for example. You spot a story about a restaurant owner who is fighting a court battle for the right to be allowed to serve burgers pink in the middle (this really happened, by the way). You make a note of the date the judge is likely to deliver a verdict and contact the media, offering to give your views on the matter.

**Other key dates in your area of expertise** like the publication of annual reports, surveys, conferences etc. As an education correspondent, for example, I diarised exam results days, the date school places were allocated and big annual international education studies like OECD and PISA.

Once you've marked up your media calendar, not only can you develop story ideas to coincide with those dates (e.g. a first person article about your relationship with your mother to run around Mother's Day or how to love Valentine's Day when you don't have anyone to love), you can also plan ahead for events you know are coming up but have an uncertain outcome e.g. budget days or court cases (along the lines of 'If the outcome is x, I can pitch an article on y').

Having a media calendar – and checking in with it daily – will not only reduce the risk of you missing out on stories, it will also help you incorporate **lead times** (i.e. the time between a journalist saying 'yes' and the story being published/broadcast) in your planning.

Monthly magazines can work three to six months ahead, weeklies five to six weeks ahead and some radio/TV programmes are made as much as a year ahead. So, if in doubt, always pitch earlier than you think you need to. It's far better to have a journalist come back and say 'this is interesting, but can you try me again in a couple of weeks?' than miss out completely.

So how do you find out the lead times for publications or programmes you want to pitch to? The easiest way is to ring up and ask. While this might sound scary, most media teams have junior staff like editorial or broadcast assistants, who should be happy to share this information with you. Just avoid calling at obviously busy times (when a radio or TV show is on air, for example) and be prepared to get passed around a bit to get the information you need.

And remember, your media calendar isn't a static thing – you should be adding to it throughout the year.

## A WORD OF CAUTION ABOUT AWARENESS DAYS

There's now an awareness day, week or campaign for everything you can possibly think of – from 'World Cancer Day' to 'Jazz Appreciation Week'. Great hook for a media story, right? Not necessarily.

There are now so many awareness days that some journalists are wary of commissioning stories around them. In fact, I've even spoken to journalists and editors who flat out refuse to cover stories hooked on awareness days. While this doesn't mean you shouldn't use awareness days to get press coverage, you will to need to work that bit harder.

The important thing to remember is that the existence of an awareness day is not a story in itself. Publish some new research, host an event or launch a campaign to *mark* an awareness day and you'll have a much better chance of getting coverage.

Let's say you work for a walking charity and want to use 'national walking day' to get some press coverage. Asking journalists to write about you simply because it's National Walking Day isn't enough. Carrying out a survey about peoples' walking habits e.g. how many parents drive their children to school or how many adults drive to the supermarket when they could walk is far more likely to interest journalists. Strong data can be also be turned into campaigns – a national campaign urging parents to leave the car at home at school run time, for example.

## 'OFF DIARY' STORIES

While you can't plan 'off diary' stories (events you can't predict), there are some practical steps you can take to increase your chances of getting coverage when they do arise.

Setting up Google Alerts using keywords in and around your area of expertise – and checking them first thing every morning – is one simple step you can take that can have a big impact on your PR.

Here are some examples that will help you understand how to find fresh angles on the stories that come up in your Google Alerts and use them to pitch ideas to the media.

Back to the walking charity example for a moment: let's say you see a news story about a school that's charging parents to drop children off in the playground (as a way of discouraging them to drive to school). You could contact a national TV news show and offer comment on the topic. You could also pitch an opinion article to an industry title or national newspaper. You could even suggest a 'how to' article for an online publication on how to get more children walking to school.

Or perhaps you're an education consultant. The story I mentioned earlier on premature babies being more likely to be unemployed as adults comes up in your Google Alert. You've been working on a campaign to make it easier for parents of premature babies to delay their child's school starting age. You could pitch an opinion article to a newspaper on the topic. You could also call a few national radio shows and say that, if they're covering the topic, you'd be happy to be interviewed.

## A QUICK WORD ON RELEVANCY

Now you might be wondering how writing something about your personal life – as I did in the example I shared at the beginning of this chapter – can help you promote your business or brand.

First off, there's usually a way to mention your business in a personal story. I didn't do it in this particular article, but I have done in others I've written on everything from my experience of miscarriage to why I wear makeup when I'm running. Secondly, even if it's not immediately apparent how you can mention your business, it's an opportunity to build a relationship with a journalist you might want to pitch more relevant ideas to in the future. Lastly, people want to do business with people. Several of my clients found me via my article on miscarriage, then came over to my website to find out more about me. If people connect with your mission and values, they generally want to know more.

## OVER TO YOU

Download my media calendar from www.janetmurray.co.uk/books and set aside a half day to create your own for the next 12 months. Not only will this help you plan your media campaigns more effectively, and incorporate lead times into your planning, you'll be amazed how many story ideas you get during the session.

# USEFUL READING

*Newsjacking: how to inject your ideas into a breaking news story and generate a ton of media coverage* by David Meerman-Scott

TELL THE
STORIES
*people*
WANT TO
HEAR
*rather than*
THE ONES
YOU
WANT TO TELL

# ≣ CHAPTER 7 ≣

# TELLING MEDIA STORIES
## PEOPLE ACTUALLY WANT TO HEAR

**H**ere's an embarrassing tale from my past.

Early in my freelance writing career, when I'd just started pitching stories into magazines and newspapers, I managed to land a lunch meeting with the editor of Healthy (one of the biggest-selling health magazines in the UK).

I wrote a lot about health at the time, and (while it might sound a bit sad), the opportunity to have lunch with the editor of a huge health magazine – and pitch her ideas over pizza – made me giddy with excitement.

I duly made lists of ideas to suggest to the editor, Heather. When the day came, after some polite chit chat, I started reeling off my list of ideas. From her polite 'hmmms' and 'yes, maybe one for the future' I could tell I wasn't hitting the spot at all. In fact, judging by Heather's body language, I was miles away.

I couldn't understand it. I'd thought really hard about the kind of stories that might work for a health magazine...so why hadn't she liked any of my ideas?

Back at home, flicking through back copies of the magazine, the penny finally dropped. Pretty much all of my story ideas had been parenting-related (my daughter was about a year old at the time), but I couldn't see a *single* story about children's health. In fact, looking at the content in more detail, it seemed to be more aimed at women without children or (judging by the fact there were a few articles on the menopause) empty nesters.

How could I have totally missed that?

I quickly regrouped and sent a fresh batch of ideas based on my new insights – several of which were accepted. And while I felt a bit embarrassed to have missed the obvious, it was a useful lesson in what editors are looking for (and what they're not).

I learned the hard way that pitching ideas I found personally interesting wasn't going to cut it. If I wanted to get editors to say 'yes' to me I needed to focus on what they were looking for i.e. content that was a perfect fit for their audience.

The biggest mistake I see newbies making is pitching the stories they want to tell rather than the ones people want to hear. It's an easy mistake to make: when you're passionate about a subject, it's tempting to think everyone else will be too, but this approach is generally PR suicide.

Making a list of ideas you find interesting, then thinking about which publications or programmes might be interested (the strategy many newbies use) is, essentially, taking potshots at success and here's why.

It may sound harsh, but journalists aren't interested in your business or brand. Or 'helping' you promote it (if you want that kind of coverage, you'll need to buy an advert). They just want great content that their audience will want to share.

And while they might be interested in covering a launch (and only then if your new book, product or service is particularly innovative or unusual), they can only do that once. I mean just how many times can you write about an app, book or beauty product...unless there's actually something new to say?

If you want to get consistent media coverage, there's no point sending out endless press releases about how brilliant your business is. You need to think more creatively.

When you start by looking at a publication or programme you want to get coverage in and think about what you could offer that would be a perfect fit for its audience, you'll have a much better chance of getting a 'yes'.

So if you've tried unsuccessfully to get PR for your business (or have found your results lacklustre), this chapter could be a game changer for you.

## GETTING STARTED WITH STORY GENERATION

I've shown you how to go after the 'low-hanging fruit' i.e. journalists who are looking for help with stories they're working on and newsjacking. Now it's time for the fun bit – generating your own story ideas.

If you've carried out the research I've suggested so far, you should now have three things:

1.  A list of target publications (ideally no more than three to five)

2.  A list of the topics they've covered recently (if it's less than a side of A4 you've probably not got enough detail).

3.  A list of headlines

The easiest way to get started is to pick one of the publications or programmes you'd like to get coverage in. Next, look at your list and identify topics that have already been covered, but you could offer a fresh 'take' on.

So let's say you're a relationship coach who is keen to get coverage in the women's magazine Red. During your research, you notice a number of practical 'how to' articles on friendship (e.g. dealing with toxic friends, what to do when you've been dumped by a friend, dealing with friends who steal your style), which suggests this is a popular topic with readers. You notice, however, that there's nothing about the different stages of friendship – an area you specialise in – so you jot down a couple of ideas around that e.g. the seven stages of friendship, the most dangerous time in a friendship, how to rescue a dying friendship and so on.

Maybe you're an accountant who specialises in working with small businesses and you'd love to get coverage in a particular national newspaper.

You notice it has a small business section every week with a 'how to' article on different aspects of running a business and many of these are listicles (i.e. list posts). While they've covered DIY tax returns, they haven't done much on outsourcing, so you jot down a couple of ideas around that e.g. 'six reasons you should outsource your accounting', 'eight questions you should ask before you hire an accountant', 'five ways hiring an accountant can save you money' and so on.

Or perhaps you'd love to get coverage in a lifestyle magazine like Stylist. You notice that in every issue they have a 'day in the life' interview with someone about their job. You notice they feature lots of business owners, so you decide to put yourself forward for that.

I like to think of it like one of those 'shape sorter' children's toys (you know – the ones where you have to put the square shape in the square hole, the rectangle shape in the rectangular hole and so on). Most people are, essentially, trying to ram a square peg into a round hole i.e. pitching the stories they want to tell rather than the ones journalists want to run. If you can show you're doing the opposite i.e. trying to find exactly the right 'shaped' content to fit the space, you'll stand out immediately.

## ADVANCED STORY GENERATION STRATEGIES

While I'd always recommend starting with the publications or programmes you want to get coverage in, I do think it's worth spending some time thinking about the stories you might have to offer. This means that when you pick up a magazine, or see a TV programme you'd like to get coverage in, you'll already have a bank of ideas to draw from. You'll just need to work out how you can shape them to fit that particular publication or programme.

## MINING YOUR LIFE FOR MEDIA CONTENT

While journalists are rarely interested in writing about your business (at least not over and over again, anyway), what they are often interested in are *the areas of your life that intersect with your business.* I talked a little about this in Chapter 7, but here are a few more examples.

Last year I wrote an opinion article for the Guardian about how I was fed up being asked to speak for free (when in most cases the people doing the asking *did* actually have the budget to pay) which stirred up quite a bit of debate. It attracted lots of shares, comments and became a talking point in various Facebook groups I belong to. A few people commented that there are some occasions when working for free is acceptable, so I followed it up a few months later with an article for Entrepreneur magazine on when it's ok to work for free.

Although these articles weren't strictly *about* my business, they allowed me to mention it. I saw a big hike in sign-ups for my free press release writing course, which is brilliant at generating leads for my consultancy and training business. And at an event I was speaking at recently, there was a lady sat in front of me who had found my website and signed up to my email list as a result of reading that very article. PR in action.

Another article I wrote – which actually had nothing to do with my business – had an even more positive impact. The article, which was about why we need to talk more about miscarriage in the workplace (and my personal experiences) was shared 10,000 times in just a few days, once again leading to a big spike in my website traffic and email sign ups. Several clients have since told me that reading that article was how they found me.

And when I realised, earlier this year, that I had two week-long overseas business trips scheduled in the space of 30 days, I pitched – and successfully placed – an article on how other mothers judge you when you travel for work. The article got a lot of attention and sent people over to my email list and Facebook group.

So instead of pitching stories *about* your business, the more you can look *around the edges of your business* – in the areas of your life that intersect with your business e.g. family, relationships, money, work and so on – the more success you're likely to have.

If you need more convincing on the value of this approach, here's a few more real-life examples.

Melanie pitched an article to the Guardian's Small Business Network about how being an expat inspired her relocation consultancy business. She has also written a series of Huffington Post articles about her experience of Danish life and culture. Melanie recently wrote another Huffington Post article about whether Danish guys are better-looking than English men, which performed well online and led to an interview with a Danish national newspaper. These articles have not only generated traffic to her website and new clients, she has also been approached by journalists from the Sunday Times and Daily Mail to be interviewed for further stories.

Cognitive behaviour therapist Claudia felt frustrated that journalists didn't want to write *about* her business – even her local newspaper. But when she pitched an article to the Daily Mail about her struggles with breastfeeding (following the publication of some new research on the topic, which she used as a hook), the editor said 'yes' pretty much by return. The following day, her local newspaper got in touch wanting to interview her.

Leadership coach Graham recognised that people weren't that interested in reading *about* his business. So he pitched a story to the Guardian's Family section about his parents separating in their eighties and how this inspired him to work as a relationship coach. The article was syndicated (i.e. bought by another media outlet) and later appeared in the Daily Mail's You magazine. Graham also did an interview with BBC Radio Scotland with a journalist who had read his article.

The great things about these kinds of articles is that they keep on giving; every time the topics I've written about lots crop up in the news e.g. miscarriage, premature birth or independent education, I know I'm bound to get a call from a journalist. I recently got a request to do a radio interview on the back of a story I wrote nearly 10 years ago.

## MANAGING YOUR FEARS

If the idea of sharing your personal life in the media makes you feel uncomfortable, please be reassured you're not alone. Many of the small business owners I work with are worried about the implications of being in the media spotlight – and rightly so.

However, I do need to give you a bit of tough love; while you don't need to reveal everything, if you're not willing to share at least some aspects of your personal life, your chances of getting media coverage will be vastly reduced.

I've worked with clients who have parenting brands but are not willing to talk about their children or share photographs of them, for example. The result? Little or no press coverage.

Others have turned down perfectly good opportunities to be featured in the media because they couldn't see how it would help their business.

Remember that talking about some aspects of your personal life in the media doesn't mean sharing everything; while I've written about my miscarriage, ectopic pregnancy, having a premature baby and being diagnosed with chronic liver disease, there are some things I wouldn't *dream* of sharing in the media. Get clear on what you're willing to share – and what you're not – from the outset and you shouldn't run into any problems.

And it doesn't all have to be personal drama; I work in a smart-looking shed at the end of my garden and have been featured in national newspapers and consumer magazines on the topic of chic sheds. Here I am in the Metro's property section talking about mine:

*"I love it because it's nothing like a conventional office, is full of my personality and just has a lovely, relaxed, homely feel about it. I've recently started using it to deliver training courses and I love that it isn't all formal and corporate, so it appeals to the kinds of people I love working with – entrepreneurs and creative business owners. It also gives me some privacy and feels more professional than working around my kitchen table."*

While the article wasn't about my business – it was about sheds – I was able to use it to (a) tell people who I am (b) tell people what I do (c) tell people what I stand for – which is what great PR is all about.

If you still feel reluctant to share anything about your personal life, here's a reality check: you can carry on sending press releases about how brilliant your business is, the award you just won or your new marketing manager, but you won't get very far. Or you can develop the kind of stories that will get you press coverage and find a way to make them work for your business.

The choice is yours.

# THE FACEBOOK TEST

If you've followed all the steps so far, you should now have a working list of ideas to pitch to your target publications (remember, at this stage, it's better to keep it manageable – say three to five).

But it's easy to get so absorbed in what you're doing, you lose sight of what might be interesting to the general public. If you're not careful, you can end up pitching ideas into the media even *you* wouldn't be interested in reading, watching or listening to.

Here's a fun strategy you can use to check if your story idea is newsworthy.

Imagine sharing your story idea on your Facebook newsfeed (that's your personal account -not a page or group).

Ask yourself these questions – honestly:

*Would people like your story?*

*Would people comment on your story?*

*Would people want to share your story?*

*Would your story divide people?*

If you think people would ignore or just 'like' your story it's probably not going to be of interest to the media. If they'd comment or share it, it may have potential. If they'd comment, share and be divided about it, you've got a winning combination.

For example, Sarah has recently written and self-published a novel with her daughter Bronte. This is interesting alone (although probably only to a regional audience or niche writing publications). The novel is loosely based on a 'real life' story – Sarah's decision to enter her daughter into a model competition to help her tackle her body image issues (Bronte was being teased at school for being too skinny). According to Bronte, strutting around in a bikini and six-inch high heels helped her gain confidence. If Sarah posted this anecdote on her Facebook page, I'm pretty sure people would comment on it. I definitely think they'd be divided on it and want to talk about the rights and wrongs of the story with their friends. So you won't be surprised to hear this story was picked up by the Mail on Sunday.

You might be thinking this strategy wouldn't work for you because you work in a niche industry and never have 'sexy' stories like that. But it's all about context. Imagine posting your story on to your Facebook account *if all your friends worked in the same industry.* I can pretty much guarantee there are ideas you'd post that some people would ignore and others people would have strong opinions on – even if they meant absolutely nothing to anyone outside of the industry.

So let's say you work in the tin mining industry, for example: changes in government regulations on conflict mineral mining might mean nothing to most people but be a big, divisive issue for those who work in the industry (that's a real example by the way).

## OVER TO YOU

Head over to www.janetmurray.co.uk/books, download my 'mining your life for media content' worksheet and set aside a couple of hours to brainstorm some ideas. Try not to get hung up on whether you would or wouldn't want to tell those stories in the media (writing them down does not mean committing to sharing them) – just get some ideas flowing.

## USEFUL LINKS

Why women need to stop working for free (Guardian)
*www.theguardian.com/women-in-leadership/2015/aug/24/show-me-the-money-why-women-need-to-stop-working-for-free*

Here's when it's ok to work for free (Entrepreneur)
*www.entrepreneur.com/article/270369*

Danish men? Hunky, humble or simply stylish (Huffington Post)
*www.huffingtonpost.co.uk/melanie-haynes/danish-men-hunky-humble-or-simply-stylish_b_9924848.html*

Mum who thought 'breast is best' developed post-natal depression (Daily Mail)
*www.dailymail.co.uk/femail/article-3253795/Mother-brainwashed-believe-breast-best-developed-post-natal-depression-bottle-feeding-newborn.html*

Mum and Dad split up in their 80s (Guardian)
*www.theguardian.com/lifeandstyle/2016/jan/30/mum-and-dad-split-up-in-their-80s*

GET THE RIGHT *IDEA* IN FRONT OF THE RIGHT *person* AT THE RIGHT TIME

# CHAPTER 8

# HOW TO FIND JOURNALISTS' CONTACT DETAILS

## (WITHOUT LOOKING LIKE A CRAZY STALKER)

One of my regular 'gigs' in recent years has been covering for the education editor at the Guardian. One of the biggest takeaways for me has been seeing how many great ideas don't get published – simply because they're sent to the wrong person.

Let me explain: as I write, the Guardian has numerous education editors. There is Richard, education editor for news; Alice, who is the education editor for features (a regular section which appears in the paper every Tuesday); and Kate, Zofia and Judy, who look after the Guardian's Schools, Higher Education and Students networks (online 'hubs' that feature content for people who are either studying or working in education). That's five different editors, who run different types of content for different audiences.

I've lost count of the times I've been sent an idea that's unsuitable for me, but might work for Richard, Kate, Zofia or Judy. If I have the time, I forward it on to them straight away. If I'm busy, I make a mental note to do it later but, eight times out of ten, I forget. My job is to populate my section with the right kind of content – not my colleagues' (who take exactly the same approach as me).

While some editorial offices communicate better than others, from my experience, this example is pretty typical. I share this story to show you how important it is to get your idea in front of the right person i.e. the journalist who can make a decision about whether to run your story. If you're not prepared to put in the time to find out who this is, you could miss out on coverage for a perfectly good idea.

## ARE MEDIA DATABASES WORTH IT?

If you're short on time, paying for a list of journalists' email addresses can be tempting. Personally I think this is a bad idea – particularly when you're starting out – especially as most journalists' email addresses can be found in a few clicks.

And in my experience, media databases are not always up-to-date and don't include the kind of information that can make all the difference to your pitching – that a particular journalist is on a short sabbatical or secondment to another desk, for example.

Using media databases can also lead to a lazy approach to PR. If you're serious about getting media coverage for your business or brand, you need to be building long-term relationships with the media. But if your idea of networking involves looking up a bunch of journalists' email addresses on a spreadsheet and blasting over a press release, you're probably not going to get very far.

While creating your own database (or getting someone to do this for you) using information from social media platforms like Twitter and LinkedIn, or just picking up the phone and asking, does mean investing a little more time upfront, it will pay off in the long-run.

## FIRST THINGS FIRST

If you're looking to get coverage in a particular publication or programme, it's generally not enough to find out the name of the editor; you need to find out the name of the person who has responsibility for the particular section or segment you're targeting.

So if you're pitching a beauty story to a women's glossy magazine, look to see if there's a beauty editor. If not try the features editor.

If you're pitching to an online publication like Entrepreneur, find out who looks after the section you think your story idea might fit into e.g. 'Make More Happen' or 'Women Entrepreneurs'.

And if you're pitching to radio or TV, find out the name of the producer for the particular programme – or programme segment – you want to pitch to. Do also bear in mind that the person you should pitch to might vary according to the *type* of story. So if you're pitching a news story to a national newspaper, you probably want either the news editor or (depending on the topic of your story) a specialist reporter e.g. the science or business correspondent.

Sadly there are no hard and fast rules. The more you can talk to journalists and find out how things work on their particular publication or programme, the better placed you'll be.

# WHERE TO LOOK FOR JOURNALISTS' CONTACTS

## 1. In the publication

Many magazines or newspapers include lists of journalists. These are generally near the front or back of the publication. Radio and TV shows often list their staff online (as do many magazines and newspapers these days).

## 2. On social media

Most journalists are on Twitter, so if you put the name of the publication or programme you're interested in, into the search bar on the top right, plus the word 'editor' 'journalist' or 'writer', then click 'accounts', you'll get a list of relevant journalists. It's usually pretty easy to work out from their biographies which is the best contact.

As I mentioned in Chapter 5, It's also a good idea to create a Twitter list of journalists on your target publications and check in daily to see what they're talking about.

Not only will you get a feel for the kind of stories they're interested in, you might even spot requests for help with stories they're working on. You can also start building a relationship by replying to their tweets and sharing their content.

A keyword search on LinkedIn can also help you find journalists working in specific roles on specific publications.

Do bear in mind that journalists often search for experts on social media. So make sure all your social media profiles are complete, with an up-to-date, good quality photo (not an Ibiza holiday snap). You should also, ideally, include a 24/7 email and/or phone number.

Use your website and social media profiles as an opportunity to 'show what you know.' If you've done any radio/TV, having a clip on your LinkedIn profile and/or your website will help a lot, as will linking to your blog or any previously published work.

## 3. By phone

This is often the quickest and most effective way to get journalists' contact details. It's also the most underused. You may get passed around a bit, but you're far more likely to get the name of the right person to send your story idea to. You might even pick up some useful nuggets of information about things like lead times (how far ahead journalists are working on stories) and what they're working on in the future.

## 4. Media enquiry databases

Get free trials of media enquiry databases like Response Source and Gorkana (and some of the other examples mentioned in Chapter 5) which connect journalists looking for sources for stories with people who want to be featured in the media. Nab the names and email addresses of relevant journalists (even if you haven't got a story to pitch them right now, you might do later). If you have the budget, you may even decide to subscribe to one of these services (I don't necessarily think they're a bad idea – I just think you shouldn't rely on them completely).

Once you've got the name of the person you need to get your idea in front of, you need to work out the correct email format. This is usually pretty easy – just find an email address for someone else who works at your target publication/programme and figure it out from there (tip: it's usually pretty easy to find email addresses for the ads sales execs.

Email hunter (emailhunter.co) and Who.is (who.is) are pretty useful too.

## WHAT ABOUT PHONE NUMBERS?

With the exception of news reporters working on breaking news, most journalists prefer email to phone. Many don't even answer their phones – particularly when they're on deadline (or 'on air' in the case of radio or TV). Don't let that put you off phoning though; just call the main switchboard of the publication or programme you're interested in and ask to be put through to the relevant person or team e.g. the 'news editor' or the 'forward planning team'. The more you're willing to get on the phone, the better you'll get at knowing who to ask for. Avoid obviously busy times and make sure you have an email outlining your idea ready to send, as most journalists will ask for one.

## OVER TO YOU

Identify five journalists you'd like to build a relationship with over the next few months. Follow them on Twitter, find out what they're talking about and get their email addresses (using some of the suggested strategies).

A NICELY WRITTEN

PRESS RELEASE

IS NO

*guarantee*

OF

PRESS
COVERAGE

# CHAPTER 9

# HOW TO WRITE AN AWESOME PITCH

## OR PRESS RELEASE

I got an email late one Friday afternoon from a guy asking how much I'd charge to write him a press release about a product he was launching on the following Monday.

I replied that I wouldn't write him a press release because I didn't think his story (or at least the way he was telling it) would be of interest to journalists. I would, however, be happy to work with him on a consultancy basis, helping him develop some ideas that *would* be of interest to journalists and help him draft a suitable pitch or press release.

He emailed back: "Can you please just tell me how much you'd charge to write the press release?"

I have several email exchanges like this every week – most often from startups in a similar predicament. I rarely get to hear what happens next. But, if my clients' experiences are anything to go by, I suspect they find someone who will take their money to write a press release no one will be interested in, then feel disappointed and disillusioned when nothing happens (many of my coaching clients come to me, in desperation, when they realise their press releases are not being picked up by journalists).

It baffles me that so many people – particularly cash-strapped startups –

are lining up to throw money at something that clearly doesn't work. That even a journalist with 15 years' experience is telling them won't work.

"Why don't you just give them what they want?" someone said to me recently. "Just write the press release, take the money and run!"

The simple answer is this: if I took money from people to write press releases I *knew* journalists wouldn't be interested in, I'd feel bad about it – as if I was taking advantage of them.

It could also be damaging to my reputation: do I really want to be known as the go-to person for writing press releases journalists don't even read? No thanks. I'd rather show people that there is another way to get media coverage – one that doesn't involve spending a fortune on press releases no one will read. And that's exactly what I'm going to do in this chapter.

## A COMMON NEWBIE MISTAKE

If you're new to PR, you may have heard that getting media coverage is all about sending press releases. If you write a press release (or get someone to do it for you), send it off to a handful of journalists, you'll open the newspaper a few days later and see a half-page story about your business or product launch.

If that's what you were thinking, I'm sorry to disappoint you, but you're going to have to work a bit harder for your media coverage.

A press release is not a media story. It is a form of communication that helps journalists decide whether or not they want to cover a story. And it's certainly no guarantee of coverage; most journalists get hundreds of press releases every day, so unless the subject line really grabs them, there's a good chance they won't even look at yours.

The bottom line is this: it doesn't matter how well written your press release is, if your story isn't interesting – and relevant to their audience – journalists won't be interested in covering it.

# SO IS IT WORTH WRITING PRESS RELEASES AT ALL?

Yes – as long as you're not relying on them solely for press coverage. Here's why:

**Many regional and industry publications and programmes are produced by small teams, with minimal resources.** This means a well-written press release can make it into print – or on air – without you even speaking to a journalist.

This doesn't mean you should just send out press releases to regional and industry titles and hope for the best. You'll still need to think carefully about each publication you're pitching to and write a tailored email pitch (more on how to do this coming up) to go with it.

**They're a handy reference for journalists.** Having a document you can refer to with key points, names and contacts – all in one place – can feel like a God-send – particularly when you're working to tight deadlines (and most journalists usually are). More on this later, but I personally think writing a tailored email pitch for each journalist you approach with a press release pasted in the body of the email below is the most effective approach.

**They give you legitimacy.** While I personally have no problem getting an informal email pitch from a 'gmail' or 'hotmail' address (in fact I rather like it), offering a story in a format that journalists are familiar with, does give you a certain level of legitimacy. Just don't let not having one stop you from pitching stories to journalists.

I've seen far too many people (small business owners in particular) miss out on press coverage because they don't have time to write a press release. If you think you've got something journalists will be interested in, just pick up the phone or dash off a quick email – they can always ask for more information if they need it.

**A press release is content.** A press release can easily be re-purposed into a news story for your website, copy for your newsletter or annual report. And, if nothing else, writing a weekly or monthly release is a way of documenting your news over the course of a year.

There's a lot of debate on whether posting press releases online can help boost your SEO. But while it seems logical to assume that the more online content there is about your business, the better, if no one is likely to use search engines to find the content in your press releases (is anyone *really* going to be searching to find out about your new marketing director, for example?), I'd question the value of doing this.

For many people, a business blog with useful content that solves peoples' problems (your ideal clients or target audience, that is) or makes their lives easier in some way is far more likely to send you soaring up the search engine rankings. And will probably save you time and money too.

**Press releases can keep you focused on your PR.** When you're busy running a business – or juggling a busy communications role – PR is often the thing that gets pushed to the bottom of your 'to-do' list. Setting yourself a target to write a fortnightly or monthly press release can keep you focused and spark story ideas – even when it feels like there's nothing new to say.

# HOW TO WRITE A PRESS RELEASE

Here are some of the most common questions I get asked about writing press releases.

### *How long should my press release be?*

The ideal length of a press release is about an A4 side (or about 3-400 words – the length of a short news story). If yours is longer than that, you've probably included unnecessary waffle that doesn't add anything to your story.

### *What information should I include in my press release?*

A press release is, essentially, a news story. So if you want to get an idea of how it's done, look no further than your daily newspaper.

Your opening line should be a summary of the story (ideally no more than 15-20 words) and read like the opening line of a news story.

Journalists are generally taught to get as many of the 5ws (who, what, where, why and when) in the opening line – so if you want examples of great first lines for press releases – look at a news story on a big news site like the BBC.

Another way of looking at it is to imagine your story is going to be covered on a TV or radio programme. A presenter generally has around five to six seconds to introduce each item – what would they say about yours? For example: 'And coming up next...the Kent business owner with the biggest olive grove in Europe...in his back garden.'

Or imagine telling a friend – one who doesn't know anything about your business – about your story idea. You'd leave out the jargon and keep it really simple. And that's exactly what you need to do for journalists.

Sub-headings and bullet points can be useful to make information easy to digest, particularly if you're including figures or statistics.

Most press releases include quotes from at least two people a 'notes to editors' section at the end, together with background and other useful information e.g. web addresses, contact details etc

## *How should I structure my press release?*

There are no hard and fast rules about how to structure a press release, but I'd suggest you include the following things, in this order:

1. A clear, compelling headline that summarises what the story is about

2. An opening line that summarises your story (ideally in no more more than 15-20 words)

3. A couple of paragraphs that outline your idea in more detail

4. A couple of quotes which provide greater insight

5. A 'notes to editors' section (with key information like web addresses, contact numbers etc)

## What kind of quotes should I include?

Quotes can be helpful for journalists (and on regional or trade publications are often used, word for word), but a common beginner's mistake is to use quotes to provide information (which has often been mentioned elsewhere in the release anyway) and include jargon and/or technical language. e.g. "Last year, we exported 1m tonnes of olives to 500 suppliers in 10 European countries."

Quotes should be used to provide insight and opinion and sound like a real person said them. e.g. "Last year, our olives were sold in 10 European countries. It's funny to think that people in France, Spain or Italy are enjoying food that was, essentially, grown in our back garden in Kent."

## Should I include my press release as an attachment?

Paste your press release underneath (a busy journalist may not bother to an open an attachment). It's also a good idea to include a short email outlining your idea (no more than a paragraph or two) and where you think it might fit in the publication or programme you're pitching to.

## Should I include photos?

Yes – if they're relevant to the story. But don't send big files as these can clog up peoples' inboxes.

## How can I make my press release stand out?

Most journalists get hundreds of press releases each day which means they may only open emails with a compelling subject line. So it's a good idea to label emails containing press releases with the phrase 'press release' or 'story idea.' A great subject line is also a must.

Don't try to be mysterious or clever; most journalists will spend just a few seconds deciding whether something looks interesting enough to read. If they don't immediately get what your story is about, they'll move onto the next thing in their inbox.

So if your story is about the the launch of the first 'men only' nail bar – say exactly that. 'Local business nails it with 'men only' service' might sound better, but will mean nothing to a busy journalist scanning through their inbox.

### *Do I need to write different version of my press release for different journalists?*

Ideally, yes. While it can be a useful background document for journalists, remember that a press release isn't a story. If you want to maximise your chances of getting press coverage, you may to tweak (rather than rewrite) your idea – and your release – for different publications or programmes.

This example is around 250 words but contains all the relevant information. The 'top line' is in the first sentence and the quotes tell a story (rather than state fact).

## UK's FIRST CEREAL CAFE TO OPEN
## IN EAST LONDON NEXT MONTH

The UK's first cereal Café will open its doors this December in Brick Lane, Shoreditch.

The Cereal Killer Café will offer 100 varieties of breakfast cereals and more than 13 kinds of milk. There will also be 20 different toppings, including honey, nuts and marshmallows. For customers who aren't so enthusiastic about cereal, the Café will also offer toast, waffles, pastries and other breakfast staples.

The cafe is the brainchild of twin brothers Alan and Gary Keery, both former pastry chefs who say they wanted to recreate the nostalgia from their childhood.

Alan Keery, co-founder of the Killer Cereal Café said: "Growing up in the 1980s we loved watching all the cereal adverts on telly – Ready Brek, Rice Krispies, Sugar Puffs – and talking about them with our friends. We even mixed them together to make our own cereal brands, named things like Corn Puffs and Weetakrispies and designed our own packaging and everything. I think a lot of people feel nostalgic about those pre-internet days too – when a new cereal was the talk of the youth club – which is where the idea came from for the café .

His brother Gary Keery said: "My favourite cereal at the minute is anything peanut butter flavoured from America, especially Cap'n Crunch Peanut Butter mixed with Strawberry Milk! And as for the classics, I am still a fan of Shreddies which is my go to comfort food when served with hot milk."

### NOTES TO EDITORS
The Cereal Café will open on Monday December 5th
For more information, contact Heather on 0207 345779 or email
heather@cerealcafe.co.uk

# HOW TO WRITE EMAIL PITCHES FOR JOURNALISTS

First off, although I've spent more time talking about press releases in this chapter (simply because they need a little bit more explanation) being able to write a great email pitch is far more important.

And here's the thing: even if you never ever ever write a press release, you can still get great media coverage for your business.

Got that? I hope so, because I really can't stress that point enough.

So here's how to write an email pitch a journalist will actually read.

1. **Label the subject header of your email.** Journalists are actively looking for great content ideas, so label your subject line with 'story idea' or 'pitch' and they're far more likely to open it.

2. **Use the subject header to 'sell' your story.** A concise subject header that summarises your story (ideally in 10 words or less) is far more likely to get a journalist's attention. Resist the temptation to use puns or clever wordplay though; an obscure headline that doesn't mean anything to a

journalist may get ignored. Let's say you're pitching a story about the new brewery you've just launched to your local newspaper (the first in your town). While you might be tempted to write something like 'Former lawyers brew up a new business idea' – this doesn't actually tell a busy journalist what your business is about. Much better to say something like 'Ex-lawyers open Gravesend's first brewery.'

3. **Skip the introductions.** When you're pitching to a new publication or programme it's tempting to give a long introduction that explains the background of your business or brand. Although this might sound harsh, journalists aren't interested in you or your business – they're interested in great content. So get straight to the point – you can fill in the background later in your pitch.

4. **Get your 'top line' in the first line of your pitch.** Summarise your story idea in the first line of your pitch (ideally in 10 words or less – you can even repeat your subject header) and you'll have a much better chance of getting journalists' attention.

5. **Use an informal, conversational style** with strong, visual imagery and examples. Imagine you're telling a friend about the idea and you should have it about right.

6. **Don't include attachments.** Post press releases in the body of an email instead. Like most of us, journalists generally aren't keen on opening attachments from people they don't know (nor do they have the time). If they want more information, they'll ask for it.

7. **Offer images if you have them.** They don't have to be professional, but they should be good quality. If you have a great picture that will really sell your story, by all means include it in your pitch – just don't send massive files.

Here is an example of an email pitch (for a local newspaper). As you can see, the email subject header is clearly labelled, the 'top line' is in the first line of the email (with the background at the bottom) and the style is conversational.

## STORY IDEA: GRAVESEND'S FIRST CRAFT BEER BREWERY OPENS IN CHURCH STREET

Hi David

I was wondering if you'd be interested in writing something on the craft beer brewery we're opening in Lord Street this week, which we believe is Gravesend's first?

To give you a quick bit of background, we're a couple of ex-lawyers (brothers, in fact) who've swapped life in a City law firm for running our own craft beer brewery. We started out making beer in the kitchen of our tiny East End studio flat – mainly for our family and friends – but when we realised our hobby had the potential to become a business, we quit our jobs, moved back in with our parents in Gravesend and decided to make a go of it.

Five years on, we've just moved into our first business premises in West Street – which was the home of Russell's brewery (one of the town's biggest breweries from the 1850s onwards). In fact you can still see their original branding on the wall outside. Our parents are delighted to get their kitchen back and we can't wait to finally have our own premises – where we're also planning to run beer-brewing courses and taster nights.

We'd love it if you could join us at our launch party on Thursday evening at 8pm. If you can't make it along, we're available for phone interviews and have some great professional photos you can use.

Look forward to hearing from you,

Lee Smith

### ABOUT US

Former lawyers Lee & Alex Smith, who both attended Gravesend High School, are the founders of Gravo Brew. You can find out more about them here www.gravobrew.com and contact them on 07965 889474 or lee@gravobrew.com. They tweet @gravobrew and their Facebook page is at GravoBrewUk.

# PITCHING JOURNALISTS OVER THE PHONE

Imagine you're working on an important piece of writing. You're under pressure because it has to be finished in exactly 20 minutes. The phone rings, and you immediately feel irritated because you're on deadline, but you pick it up anyway, because that's your job. The person at the other end doesn't even stop to introduce themselves or ask if you have time to chat – they just start talking. You're trying to make sense of what they're saying, but you're struggling to keep up because your head is still in the piece of writing you've been working on. And they just keep talking and talking, barely pausing for breath. By the time they finally stop and say 'so does that sound interesting?' you're so irritated you just want to get them off the phone as quickly as possible.

This is exactly how most journalists feel when you call them up with a story idea. It's not because they're being awkward or difficult; it's because their job is pretty pressurised.

While you know your story inside out, when you call to tell them about it, they're hearing it for the very first time. This means they're having to work harder to process what you're saying. And because you're nervous, you're probably talking far too fast, which makes it even harder for them to keep up.

While most journalists generally prefer email, if your story is particularly timely, there will be times when it's better to call.

Here's some pointers to help you deliver a great phone pitch.

**Always ask if the journalist has time to talk –** not only is this polite, it also forces you to slow down and wait for an answer, which will stop you gabbling. If they say no, ask when would be a better time and call them back then.

**State what you want** by saying something like 'do you have time to discuss a story idea?' or 'I've got a story idea to run past you – do you have a few minutes?'

**State who you are (but don't overdo it).** I've been on the receiving end of so many phone pitches where the person has been so nervous, they've forgotten to introduce themselves. A quick 'It's Heidi Smith here, I run a bakery in Soho' or 'My name's John Webber, I'm a child psychologist' should be enough.

Avoid long jargon-filled job titles like 'I'm the CEO and research director of a leadership and organisational change consultancy' as these will mean nothing to a busy journalist (if you need tips on how to describe what you do, see the tips on writing your LinkedIn description in chapter 5 )

**Don't give the context or 'background' to your story.** Just get straight to the point.

**Have your 'top line' (ideally in ten words or less) prepared before you get on the phone.** Get straight into your pitch – just as you would on email e.g. 'I was wondering if you'd be interested in an article on *whether it's worth creating an app for your business?*' or 'I was wondering if you'd be interested in an opinion article *on why too much sleep can be bad for you?*' In both those cases, the 'top line' is ten words or less. If you can't say what you need to say in less than ten words, your pitch probably needs some work.

**Don't say 'I'm calling on behalf of'.** Remember what I said in Chapter 1 about journalists finding PRs annoying (harsh, but true)? That's why opening a phone pitch with 'I'm calling on my behalf of my client xxxx' is PR suicide.

To put it into context, I do a bit of pro bono PR for local community groups I'm involved in. But I wouldn't dream of getting on the phone to a reporter and saying 'I'm calling on behalf of the team at Shorne Woods Country Parkrun as I have a story idea for you...'. I'd say 'are you interested doing something on the couple who are getting married at the parkrun on Saturday?' I'm sure I don't need to tell you which is more likely to get a journalist's attention.

Just because someone is paying you to do their PR, doesn't mean you have to go all dull and corporate. So instead of saying 'I'm calling on behalf of', just get straight to the story. 'I was wondering if you'd be interested in doing something on *a new app that pays your utility bills for you*' or 'I was wondering if you'd be interested in doing something o*n the new gender neutral doll for children that's being launched next week?*' Get them interested in the story first – you can fill in the background later.

## IF THEY SAY 'YES'

When you get a 'yes' from a journalist, it's tempting to hang up and do a victory dance around your office. Try to keep your cool. Don't hang up until you've got all the information you need e.g. deadlines, what kind of copy and/or images they need and agree when and how you will get this to them.

## IF THEY SAY 'NO'

Don't argue or try to persuade them. Simply ask if there's anything else you can help them with at the moment. If they're looking for help with a specific story, expert or case study, it could be your chance to start building a relationship.

## IF THEY ASK YOU TO CALL BACK

If they're busy, or on deadline, they might say something like 'sounds interesting, but can you call me back later?' If this happens, find out *exactly* when they want to you to call back and on what number. And make sure you do.

## OVER TO YOU

Head over to www.janetmurray.co.uk/books to get my free templates for writing pitches and press releases. Draft an email pitch to a journalist using the tips and strategies outlined in this chapter.

THERE IS

# NO

SUCH THING AS

*'set & forget'*

# PR

## ≡ CHAPTER 10 ≡

# WHERE (AND WHEN) TO SEND YOUR PITCH
## OR PRESS RELEASE

O ne of the most common questions I get asked about PR is: 'should I use a distribution service to send out my press release?' For the uninitiated, this is where you pay a company (or individual) who has access to a database of journalists' contacts to send it out for you, which you can do for as little as a few hundred pounds.

Personally, I think this is bad idea. Here's why:

1. It doesn't matter how many journalists you send it out to – if your story isn't newsworthy, they won't use it

2. Media databases can be out of date or missing those vital titbits of information that can make all the difference to your pitch e.g. x journalist is on maternity leave or y journalist is taking a sabbatical

3. PR success – like any aspect of your business – is really about building relationships. So if your idea of 'networking' is sending a blanket press release to hundreds of journalists whose names you don't even know, you're not going to get very far

Sadly there is no such thing as 'set and forget' PR. If you're serious about getting press coverage, you need to invest time researching the publications and programmes you'd like to be featured in (which I explain how to do in chapter 4) identify the relevant editors to approach with your ideas and start building relationships with them.

If you've followed all the steps I've laid out so far, you should be starting to build up your own database of journalists' contact details (if you need to go back over this, it's in chapter 8) so you can make sure you get your idea in front of the right person.

## WHEN IS THE BEST TIME TO SEND YOUR PITCH OR PRESS RELEASE?

The rather unsatisfactory answer to this is 'it depends.' If you're pitching an idea to a daily newspaper or programme, it's a good idea to get in touch before the morning conference (the daily meeting where journalists pitch story ideas to their editors). But timings vary on different publications and programmes and you may find some content – particularly more indepth features – are commissioned weeks ahead. So it really all comes down to knowing your target publications and programmes inside out – and doing the level of research I outlined in Chapter 4).

## SHOULD YOU SEND THE SAME IDEA TO DIFFERENT JOURNALISTS?

This is another rather unsatisfactory 'it depends'. If you have a really great news story the kind you can imagine seeing reported in different publications and programmes – (e.g. you've discovered a potential cure for cancer or carried out research that shows women are better drivers than men, for example) you might want to pitch it to a news agency like the Press Association, Reuters or Associated Press (or the equivalent in your part of the world).

News agencies gather news reports and sell them to subscribing organisations, such as newspapers, magazines and radio and television broadcasters. So if you pitch – and successfully place – a story with a news agency, your story will go directly onto the editorial systems (commonly referred to as the 'news wire') on all the major national and regional media. This can work well, and save you a lot of time. The only downside is, once your pitch or press release is accepted by the news agency, you don't have any control over whether journalists pick it up or not.

The reality for most businesses and brands, is that big news stories don't come along every week, so most of the time you'll probably have more luck going direct to journalists. This is where it gets tricky; journalists love exclusives, so unless it's a news story with wide appeal (like the examples mentioned above) if you pitch them an idea, then they see the same story reported elsewhere, they may not be too pleased.

Unless your idea is really timely, it's generally best to pitch journalists one at a time and wait for an answer before moving onto the next one. And don't make the mistake of thinking it's acceptable to pitch the same story to different journalists on the same publication or on the 'Sunday' version of a newspaper. Although unlikely, it's not impossible that two journalists could end up covering the same story and imagine how embarrassing that would be for everyone involved.

Of course you can't sit around forever waiting for journalists to come back to you, so the best advice I can give you is to be completely transparent about who else you're talking to.

## FOLLOWING UP YOUR PITCH OR PRESS RELEASE

If you've sent out your pitch or press release, and you haven't heard anything back – don't panic – this is perfectly normal when you're starting out on your PR journey (in fact, it's perfectly normal, even for seasoned pros).

So what should you do about it?

First off, if you haven't heard anything after a few days (or hours if it's a particularly timely story), it's perfectly fine to send a follow up email. I'd suggest forwarding your initial email with a polite 'just wondering if you'd had a chance to have a look at this yet?' It's also fine to phone – just avoid obviously busy times like press day (for print publications) or when a show is on air (for radio or TV).

But if you've chased a few times – and not had a reply – it's probably safe to assume your story isn't of interest. It's also reasonable to try the story elsewhere. And this is where the real work begins.

Working out what might have gone wrong – and what you can learn from the experience – is *so* important and will improve your chances of getting a 'yes' next time (or with another journalist if you plan to try the story elsewhere).

In my experience, these are five common reasons journalists ignore pitches or press releases, which I explain here. I also share tips on what you can learn from the experience.

### 1. The idea wasn't suitable for the publication/programme

**How to improve:** Go back and look at the publication or programme you pitched to. Who is their target audience? What kind of content do they normally run? How close was your idea to the typical content? Asking yourself questions like this should help you identify the 'missing' piece.

### 2. The subject header wasn't compelling enough

**How to improve:** Go back and look at your email subject header? Did you label the subject header 'press release' or 'pitch' (if not, you should have)? Would your subject header mean anything to someone who hadn't heard about the story before? Have you used puns or wordplay (these are best avoided)? Ask yourself if there is anything that might have stopped a busy journalist opening your email.

### 3. You didn't send your idea to the right person

**How to improve:** Go back and look at the email address you used. Did you send your idea to a generic email address e.g. ideas@janetmurray.co.uk (this is a bad move)? Did you check to see who looked after the particular section you were pitching to? Use Twitter and LinkedIn to double check your contact information.

## 4. You got your timing wrong

**How to improve:** Think about when you sent your press release. Did you contact the journalist on the morning of your launch (meaning they wouldn't have had enough time to turn the story round, even if they were interested). Did you pitch a story about your event *after* it happened? (journalists aren't generally interested in 'old news'). Or maybe it was a nice idea but there wasn't a 'hook' (when they get a pitch or press release, journalists will always ask themselves: why do people need to hear about this now?')

## 5. You took too long to get to the point

**How to improve:** Go back and look at your press release or email pitch. Did you include a long, rambling introduction about your business? Did you 'bury' your story at the end of your pitch or press release? Did you attach your press release instead of pasting it into the body of your email? Journalists generally make a decision whether they're interested in a story within seconds...so if you don't grab their attention in the first sentence, you've probably already lost them.

In my experience, in the vast majority of cases the problem is Number 1 – the quality of the idea.

Sometimes it's a case of tweaking things slightly and re-pitching. Other times you have to hold your hands up, admit your idea is pants and go back to the drawing board. But taking responsibility for the problem and asking yourself tough questions like these is never wasted time. Even if this attempt is beyond rescue, you'll learn valuable lessons that will help you nail your next pitch.

# OVER TO YOU

If you completed the task at the end of Chapter 9, check your email pitch against the five common reasons journalists say no. Head over to www.janetmurray.co.uk/books to get my cheat sheet on chasing up pitches and press releases.

IF YOU HAVE
HANG-UPS
ABOUT YOUR
WRITING
you're
PROBABLY A BETTER
writer
THAN YOU
THINK

# ⹌ CHAPTER 11 ⹌

# SOULFUL WRITING

S o you've pitched an idea to a newspaper, magazine or online publication and the editor has said 'yes'.

The trouble is, you've now got to write the bloomin' thing. And it's sent you into full-on panic mode.

Sound familiar? If so, you're not alone.

I've yet to meet anyone who doesn't feel nervous about writing for a new publication or in a style they're not used to. And that includes award-winning writers.

I'll let you into another secret: those writers and columnists you admire – you know, the ones with columns in glossy magazines or stylish Sunday supplements. They don't always deliver polished copy. In fact, some deliver clunky, awkward-sounding prose that needs skilful editing before it's fit for publication.

And from my own experience of working as an editor, I've noticed something interesting: the people with the highest opinion of their writing tend to deliver the worst copy.

So if you have a few hang-ups about your copy, you're probably a better writer than you think.

In this chapter, I'll run you through the key things you need to know about writing for the media. But first, a few words about writing for the web.

## WRITING FOR THE WEB

One of the most common questions I get asked when I'm delivering writing training is this:

'Do you have any tips on writing for the web?'

I find this question baffling and here's why. There's a good chance you're reading this book on your phone or a mobile device. And even if you aren't, I'd put money on the fact you're multi-tasking: watching television, checking social media updates or texting your friends in between reading sections of this book.

Even if you're 100 per cent focused right now, I bet you've multi-tasked today: checking Facebook over breakfast, reading emails during a meeting or watching television while you shop online.

So you won't be surprised to hear that most people don't read copy, word-for-word any more. They skim and scan instead, often on their phone or a mobile device. And as as most of the copy you produce these days will end up online, in my opinion, there is no such thing as 'writing for the web' – there's just good and bad writing.

With that in my mind, here are some general tips you can apply to everything you write for the media.

## KEEP IT SIMPLE

This means short words, sentences and paragraphs. No complex or technical vocabulary. And no 'word waste' (that's anything that doesn't add meaning or insight).

Choose strong verbs, use adjectives sparingly and your writing will have more 'bite'.

To put it into context, it's the difference between this:

*The keen sharp spike of pleasure when I make something new and that all-consuming feeling continues to drive me to explore more.*

and this:

*Cooking excites me.*

Let every word work for its place on the page. Just as it should do.

# BREAK IT UP

According to latest research from the University of Western Ontario, Canada, the average attention span is now just eight seconds.

So break up your text with bullet points, sub-headings and images and add value with hyperlinks to both your own content (if it makes editorial sense – journalists will cut anything that looks like it's just a plug for your business) and other useful sources.

# USE THE ACTIVE VOICE

Note the difference between these two sentences:

*The newspaper is being read by the girl* (passive voice)

and

*The girl is reading the newspaper* (active voice)

The second is more engaging because the *subject* of the sentence (i.e. the girl) is performing the action stated by the verb (reading the newspaper). It's also more direct and uses less words.

# AVOID JARGON/TECHNICAL LANGUAGE

Work on the principle that people generally know less than you think they do about any given topic and you shouldn't go far wrong.

# START WITH A STORY

When I'm working as a commissioning editor, I often send copy back to writers and say something like this: 'can you start with a story?' or 'can you put some people in it?'

Why? Because people love stories, especially if you give them unanswered questions and hint at unexpected twists and turns.

I think you can make any subject interesting if you put people centre stage (and believe me, I've had to write about some pretty dull subjects over the years) and treat them like characters in a novel.

Take this example from this **Salon** article: **The day I left my son in the car**.

*The day it happened was no different from most; I was worried, and I was running late. I was worried because in a few hours' time I was going to be enduring a two-and-a-half hour flight with my kids, ages one and four. I was running late because, like many parents of small children, I often find there just aren't enough hours in the day.*

'The day it happened was no different from most' is a big fat hint that something awful is going to happen (something awful *does* happen, by the way, but not what you're expecting) and the uneasy sentence structure that follows sets up the mood.

And this is not just a technique you can use for first person articles. When I'm writing an opinion article, I'll often start with a story. For example, I opened a Guardian article on why we need to talk more about miscarriage with this:

*A week after my first miscarriage, I drove 140 miles from my home in Kent to Stratford-upon-Avon for a two-day conference. Although my heart was aching – and my body too – staying at home wasn't an option. Women had miscarriages every day of the week, didn't they? I couldn't sit at home feeling sorry for myself.*

*Over a gala dinner, I drank too much wine and poured my heart out to the woman to my right – a mother of four who listened kindly and patted my arm as I struggled to hold back tears. Later on, I dropped it into conversation with a male colleague.*

*"I've just had a miscarriage."*

*"I'm sorry to hear that," he said, not unkindly, but quickly moved the conversation on.*

Landing readers straight in the action like this not only draws people in, it also helps you resist the temptation to start your article by setting the scene or explaining the context (an approach that can kill your writing).

## CIRCLE BACK AT THE END

If you find yourself stressing about how to end an article, circling back at the end i.e. revisiting the characters or events you mention in the opening paragraph can be effective. I did this at the end of my article on miscarriage at work.

*'Looking back, I know I wasn't unprofessional to share my loss to colleagues. We need to start a conversation on how we talk about miscarriage – both in the workplace and outside.'*

Now I wouldn't claim for a minute that this is prize-winning prose – far from it in fact – but it does draw the article to neat close and issue a call-to-action (another little trick you can use to conclude – particularly in opinion articles).

## A WORD ABOUT OPINION ARTICLES

A good opinion article should make one single point. There may be other supporting arguments, but by the time the reader gets to the end of your article, they should have one clear, 'takeaway' point e.g 'women should say no to working for free' or 'piercing babies' ears should be banned.'

It sounds obvious, but opinion articles need to contain just that: opinion. When I'm working as an editor, one of the most common mistakes I see people making is sitting on the fence (phrases like 'it could be argued that' or 'on the one hand' are a dead giveaway). Another common error is writing everything you know about a topic rather than offering an opinion.

Remember that when people turn to the opinion section in a newspaper or magazine, they're not looking for a Wikipedia entry. They're looking for something they can connect with emotionally – something that will make them feel surprised, frustrated or even cross.

The best opinion articles evoke an emotional reaction in readers and may even make them question their own opinions e.g. 'Why can't I get sterilised in my twenties' or 'Why I love my dog more than my son'.

Remember also that an opinion article isn't an opportunity for you boast about your business. It's a chance to position yourself as a thought leader – which is far more powerful than any advert. So don't waste words on self-congratulatory PR puff about how wonderful you are – say something interesting instead. And don't forget to use statistics and research to back up your argument.

While it can vary, a typical opinion article is pretty short – often around 600-800 words. So don't spend the first couple of paragraphs giving the background or context. Open with a bold statement, story or piece of dialogue that sets out your position. End with something readers can ponder.

And do bear in mind that an editor commissioning you to submit an opinion article is no guarantee they will run it. You may have an interesting idea, but use dull, flabby prose – or fail to express an opinion – and your article could get spiked. If you're not used to sharing your opinion in the media – making a bold statement can seem scary, but the reality is this: if you can't deliver the goods, the editor won't run your article.

## OVER TO YOU

Developing a daily writing habit is the quickest way to grow your confidence as a writer. Commit to writing every single day – ideally before you doing anything else. Try the five minute journal (www.intelligentchange.com /products/the-five-minute-journal) or Daily Diary www.dailydiary.com. *The Artist's Way* by Julia Cameron is also a great read.

# USEFUL LINKS

The day I left my son in the car (Salon)
*www.salon.com/2014/06/03/the_day_i_left_my_son_in_the_car*

We need to talk about miscarriage (Guardian)
*www.theguardian.com/women-in-leadership/2015/oct/14/baby-loss-awareness-week-we-need-to-talk-about-miscarriage*

THE BEST
*stories*
ARE USUALLY AROUND
THE EDGES
OF YOUR BUSINESS

# ⧎ CHAPTER 12 ⧎

# HOW TO 'PR' A PRODUCT LAUNCH

At least once a week I get an email from someone with a book, app or product to launch wondering if I can help them get press coverage. I'm pretty confident I could – if their launch wasn't days away (which is usually the case). And while it's never impossible to get media coverage, if you're launching something, you do really need to strike when it's brand spanking new.

As you should now be aware, monthly magazines can work three to six months ahead, weeklies five to six weeks ahead and some radio/TV programmes are made as much as a year ahead. So as journalists aren't generally interested in covering 'old news', if you leave your PR efforts until a few days before your launch, you've probably left it too late.

If you're serious about about getting media coverage for a new book, product or service, you need to start your PR campaign weeks – if not months – before your launch.

You'll also need to do more than send a press release – which is is both the most common – and least effective – way to get media coverage around a launch. Essentially, it's like throwing a pack of playing cards up in the air and hoping they land where you want them to. Some might, but most won't.

And do you really want to leave your PR to chance?

Do be aware that unless your product or service is really unusual or 'disruptive' (e.g. the taxi-hailing service Uber or a novel like 50 Shades of Grey), journalists may not be be interested in writing a news story on it. But there's plenty of other kinds of media coverage you can go for.

To give yourself the best possible odds of getting press coverage, you need to take a much more strategic approach. Here's five things you can do to generate press coverage for your next launch.

## 1. Invite journalists to review your product/service

Sending out a press release (or even just an email) to journalists inviting them to review your product or service – along with a sample – is one strategy you can use to get media coverage.

Sadly it's often the least effective and here's why.

Journalists get sent tons of press releases – along with samples and review copies – every single day of the week. During a brief stint at a parenting magazine, I couldn't believe the amount of stuff that was sent to the office each day: books, beauty products, pushchairs, car seats – it seemed never-ending. At another publication I worked on, review copies of books were used to prop up wonky table legs and beauty samples often ended up in the staff loo. The Guardian holds annual 'swag auctions', where freebies and review products are gathered up and auctioned to raise money for charity. So I don't want to sound pessimistic, but the odds of your product landing on the right person's desk at the right time aren't high.

It's also worth bearing in mind that many publications and programmes plan weeks or months ahead, which means your product can be old news before it even arrives in the office (and journalists hate old news). At a recent event I held in London, the features editor of Psychologies magazine explained that editorial themes were decided months in advance (which is typical of women's glossy magazines). So it doesn't matter how brilliant your new handbags are, if your target publication isn't 'doing' handbags over the next few months, you're not going to get a look in.

This doesn't mean you shouldn't try to secure product reviews – you absolutely should – just be aware that it's a scattergun approach. And this is probably the only time you'll ever hear me say something like this, but it's a numbers game. When it comes to product reviews, the more publications and programmes you can approach, the better.

Do your research first though; some publications don't do product reviews, so sending a pitch or press release can be a complete waste of your time. And don't discount bloggers; getting reviews on popular blogs in your area of expertise may actually be more effective than traditional media coverage.

While sending a press release can work well for a product launch, do 'top' it with a short, tailored email pitch. Not all publications and programmes approach reviews in the same way; some prefer to get their own journalists to 'road test' products and write about them, some might have a list of set questions or themes and others might want you to submit your own copy (that's the word journalists generally use for writing, by the way).

The more you can show that you've looked at the publication or programme and thought about how you can help create content that's a good fit, the better chance you'll have of getting a 'yes'.

## 2. Share something interesting

People love personal stories, so instead of pitching journalists *about* your product, look for inspiration in the areas of your life that intersect with your business (there's lots of examples in chapter 7). This is a technique commonly used by authors. For example, when chick lit author Adele Parks publishes a new novel, you often see a first-person article (otherwise known as a 'confessional') in the press – usually on a topic that relates to the theme of her book e.g. being divorced by a friend or being proposed to nine times. At the end of the article there's a big juicy mention of her book and where to buy it.

## 3.Teach something

There's a growing appetite for content that teaches people a concept or skill (otherwise known as 'how to'). For example, Colin was looking for a way to promote his podcasting training and consultancy business. Instead of trying to get journalists to write about his business, I encouraged him to pitch an article to the Guardian's Small Business Network about how starting a podcast can help you market your business. He got a 'yes' pretty much by return.

Gwen wanted to promote her children's sleep app (which is designed to help kids with their bedtime routine). Instead of trying to get journalists to write about her app, I encouraged her to pitch articles on how small businesses can develop apps (and whether it is worth the investment). Gwen was also successful.

Remember Melanie – the Copenhagen-based relocation consultant? Her Huffington Post article on how to bring the Danish concept of 'hygge' (which roughly translates as 'cosy') into your home, wherever you happen to be in the world, is a great way to show her expertise and promote her business at the same time.

Do bear in mind that you don't necessarily have to teach something: it could simply be sharing the lessons you've learned from a particular experience (e.g. starting your own business or losing 20 pounds). The key thing is that the audience can (a) relate to your experience and (b) take away some actionable points.

## 4. Say something interesting

Pitching opinion articles can be a clever way to get media coverage for your product. Let's say you've written a book on failings in the education system, for example. Pitching an opinion article on something related to the topic of the book can be a great way to get a plug for your product.

For example, Nathalie – an app developer – successfully pitched an article to a national newspaper arguing that it's easy for women to get on in the tech industry (which is exactly the opposite of what you usually hear on the subject). In it she talks about her own experience – providing an effective, but subtle, opportunity to promote her own app.

## 5. Do something interesting

Sadly the fact you are launching something new isn't always enough to get journalists interested in covering your new product/service. Holding an unusual event to mark your launch can be a clever way round this problem. Think silent disco or tropical ice-skating (OTT but hopefully you get the picture).

You can even do a survey or commission some research on a topic that relates to your new product or service. For example, Danny used Google Consumer Surveys (for less than $100) for research on parents taking their children out of school for term-time holidays, which led to great national coverage for a client in the travel industry. If you're going to use research to get press coverage, just remember that you need to generate data that will be of interest to the general public (remember the 'Facebook test from Chapter 7?). It sounds obvious, but I've seen plenty of people waste money on surveys that are only of interest to people in their business.

The key thing to remember is that while journalists (particularly on the nationals) may not be interested in writing or broadcasting *about* your new book, product or service, there are plenty of creative ways to get it featured in the media. You'll still get your desired outcome – a 'mention' for your business or brand – you just need to take a different route.

# A WORD ABOUT DOING PR FOR EVENTS

Here's my 10 word top line on events PR (well, it's nine actually): *if your event is boring, journalists won't cover it.*

That's why the best time think about PR is *before* you start choosing venues, booking events/product launches, speakers or organising your catering. And the more unusual your event is, the more likely you are to get media coverage.

This is why I had no trouble getting coverage (newspaper and radio) for the group ultra marathon fundraiser I organised last year. (Have you ever heard of a group ultra marathon? Exactly).

The first women's marathon in the UK got great media coverage for exactly the same reasons – it was both new and a 'first.'

So the question you need to ask yourself is: 'What could we do at our event that's never been done before?'

It could be hosting it in an unusual venue (think heavy metal concert in a church) , at an unusual time (8am rave anyone?) or in an unusual way (how about that silent disco?).

As these examples show, contrasts and collisions (i.e. putting two unlikely things together) naturally attract media interest – which will make it much easier for you to get PR.

If you're reading this and you've already started planning your event...don't despair. Just ask yourself what you could *do* (or even *say* – more on that later) at your event that is new or unusual.

And there are plenty of creative ways to get press coverage for your event. Here's a few ideas:

**Pitch an opinion article** on a topic that relates to your business or event. For example, when I was planning my annual Soulful PR Live event, I noticed I was stressing about having too many men in my speaker lineup – so I pitched an article to the Guardian about why I believe we shouldn't boycott all-male speaker panels.

**Pitch a 'first-person' article** that tells the story of your business or event. For example, if you left your job in the city to set up a company that offers wine-tasting tours, you could pitch a first person article about that (I clocked an article exactly like this in the Daily Express recently).

**Pitch a 'how to' article** that relates to your event. I've written articles for the Entrepreneur (and the Guardian) on every aspect of PR: from how to write press releases to excuses people make not to do PR to how to do radio/TV interviews, all of which send people over to my website where they check out my events.

**Pitch stories to journalists about the things your speakers will *say* at your event**. During my time writing education stories for the Guardian, I noticed how the trade unions and school leadership organisations were brilliant at doing this. Ahead of their big conferences, they'd feed journalists a 'line' about something their head honcho was going to say in their speech e.g. 'exams are getting easier' or ' behaviour in schools is driving teachers out of the profession' and journalists would write stories about it.

In one memorable example, the head of the Girls' School Association (a UK-wide membership organisation for girls' schools) was all over the press talking about how 'young women couldn't have it all' (i.e. a career and a family).

What was interesting about this strategy was that the 'line' that was reported in the media was often just a short section or paragraph in a very balanced speech, but the clever PR people knew it was no good giving journalists 'vanilla' lines about how wonderful teachers were or how bright the future was for young people. To get journalists interested – and people talking about their event – it needed to be something people actually had an opinion on.

If you run a small business, you may be wondering how you can apply this to what you do. This is where you need to think creatively. Let's say you're running an event for small business owners on social media; while journalists may not be interested in writing about your video marketing workshop or Twitter tactics seminar, if your keynote speaker will be saying that most small business owners are wasting their time on social media, being ripped off by SEO agencies or being stung by the government for levies or taxes, for example, a reporter on a trade or regional publication might be interested.

## OVER TO YOU

Write down at least five story ideas for a launch you've got coming up, using the strategies in this chapter.

## USEFUL LINKS

The power of podcasting in business (Guardian)
*www.theguardian.com/small-business-network/2015/nov/09/break-through-noise-power-podcasting-business*

How to bring Danish hygge into your home this winter (Huffington Post)
*www.huffingtonpost.co.uk/melanie-haynes/how-to-bring-danish-hygge-to-your-home_b_8344886.html*

Parents prepared to pay fines for taking their children out of school during term time (Independent)
*www.independent.co.uk/news/education/education-news/almost-half-of-parents-prepared-to-pay-60-fines-for-taking-their-children-on-holiday-during-term-a6963981.html*

There are so many opportunities for women in tech. Why aren't there more of us? (Guardian)
*www.theguardian.com/women-in-leadership/2016/apr/04/there-are-so-many-opportunities-for-women-in-tech-so-why-arent-there-more-of-us*

Google Consumer Surveys
*www.google.com/insights/consumersurveys*

BE

*prepared*

TO EARN **YOUR**

STRIPES

# CHAPTER 13

# LANDING A REGULAR COLUMN IN A NEWSPAPER
## OR MAGAZINE

**W**ould you love to have your own column in a magazine or newspaper? Thought so. Most people I work with say exactly the same.

And while I totally believe this is possible for you, I feel I should give you a reality check.

Editors don't generally hand out regular columns to people they haven't heard of or worked with before. Most have regular contributors – professionals who write for a living – or experts they've worked with for years. So why would they take a chance on someone new?

This not to say it's impossible – of course it isn't – but if you're expecting to land a column off the back of a speculative email or two, you could be sorely disappointed.

While you do hear the odd story of people (usually those who've already attracted media attention) who've been invited to write a column, most people get there through hard work and persistence.

So if you do want to get your own column, these are the kinds of things you should be doing:

## RESEARCH, RESEARCH… AND MORE RESEARCH

If you want to become a columnist for a specific newspaper or magazine the single most important thing you can do is *read it*. And I don't mean a quick flick through; I mean studying it in detail, over a number of issues, so you can get a feel for its audience and the kind of content the editor typically runs.

Pay particular attention to the regular columnists. What kind of expertise do they have? How often are they writing for the publication? What kind of topics are they writing about? Are there any gaps i.e. topics that might interest the audience, but aren't currently being covered?

Spend some time thinking about the audience. What type of people do you think read the publication (the clues are usually in the content)? Why do they read it (are they hoping to be entertained, informed, inspired…or something else entirely)? When do they read it (at the office, on their daily commute, over a lazy weekend breakfast?)

All of this will help you get a sense of the kind of content that might work for that publication.

## START SMALL

While there's no reason you can't 'cold' pitch yourself as a columnist, it's generally much easier if you've already written a few pieces for the publication. Not only will the editor know – first-hand – that you can string a sentence together, they'll also have an idea of what you're like to work with (i.e. whether your file your copy on time, how you respond to their editing suggestions and so on).

This is why I generally advise people to start by pitching a few one-off articles, before pitching a series or column.

Starting small may also mean getting some experience as a columnist on an industry or regional title before approaching the nationals (where there is generally more competition). And approaching a national title when you're already an established columnist (and have a string of cuttings to prove it) will give you a lot more clout.

## HOW TO PITCH A COLUMN

If you're pitching a column, I'd take exactly the same approach I outlined in Chapter 9. The only thing I'd suggest you do differently, is make sure you pitch a number of ideas. A commissioning editor will want to feel reassured you have enough topics for your column to keep people interested over a number of weeks, months or even years.

## MEET JOURNALISTS IN PERSON

If you've got an idea for a column, chatting it through with an editor – rather than sending a 'cold' pitch – can be easier. But as you've already heard, getting a journalist to agree to meet for coffee or lunch can be hard. So if you can't get them to agree to a meeting, you need to find out where they're hanging out and get yourself there.

## OVER TO YOU

Identify a publication you'd love to land a column in. Does it already have a regular columnist (or columnists?) What are they writing about? Are there any gaps you could fill? What can you offer that no one else can? e.g. vegan cooking tips for people with food intolerances (because you run a restaurant that specialises in exactly that), strategies for dyslexic writers (because you're a dyslexic poet) or fashion wisdom for women over forty (because you have a blog on that topic). The more you can position yourself as the only person who can create that content, the better chance you'll have of getting a 'yes.'

# BE
# VISUAL
## EVEN FOR
# RADIO

# CHAPTER 14

# HOW TO SOUND GREAT ON AIR

## MEDIA INTERVIEW SKILLS

A few months back, I got a phone call from a TV researcher on a daytime chat show called the Alan Titchmarsh show. She'd read an article I'd written on the topic of fee-paying schools (remember I mentioned it was quite a controversial topic in the UK?) and was wondering if I'd be interested taking part in their 'Daily Ding Dong' segment, which pits two opposing arguments against one another. I'd never been on the Alan Titchmarsh show before, and thought it sounded fun, so I said I was.

Now when you get a call from TV or radio researcher, it doesn't mean you're definitely going on the show; often they are just sounding you out to see what your views are, what you sound like and how you'd fit with the guests they've already booked.

The conversation went well, but I was so distracted by the thought of being on telly, I forgot one of the questions I always tell my clients to ask: 'Who will I be on with?'

Fifteen minutes into the conversation, I finally remembered.

'Katie Hopkins,' said the researcher.

For the uninitiated, Katie Hopkins is a TV personality and newspaper columnist. She first appeared on the reality game show The Apprentice (where aspiring entrepreneurs compete for £250,000 investment from British business magnate Alan Sugar) and is known for her offensive views, including ' To call yourself plus size is just a euphemism for being fat' and 'Ginger babies. Like a real baby, but so much harder to love.'

She's personally insulting to anyone she comes into contact with (at least on radio and TV) and it's difficult to take any conversation she's involved in seriously. So while it would have been a good story to tell my friends down the pub, I couldn't see how appearing on the show was going to be helpful to my business or brand.

I suddenly 'remembered' I had a prior appointment and that was the end of that.

Giving radio and TV interviews can be a great way to promote your business – and can be incredible fun – but if you don't have much experience of the media, the experience can be nerve-racking.

I've made hundreds of media appearances over the years – and trained dozens of people to do the same. In this chapter, I'll share my best tips for preparing for and delivering media interviews – and making sure you get invited back again.

## BEFORE THE INTERVIEW

Before you agree to a radio or TV interview it's important to get as much information as possible about what will happen before, during and afterwards.

Ask these questions before you agree to an interview, and you shouldn't go far wrong.

*'Why are you doing this story now?'*

A discussed in Chapter 6, journalists often talk about the 'hook' for a story i.e. the reason why they want to cover a particular story at a particular time. Knowing why a journalist or producer wants to cover a story will help you decide whether you want to do the interview.

Let's say you run a private tutoring firm and you've been contacted by a national radio show requesting an interview on the topic. When you ask the producer why she's doing the story, she says it's due to a new report that suggests some private tutoring firms are ripping off their clients. This doesn't mean you shouldn't do the interview – if you're confident that your company offers value-for-money, it's a great opportunity to promote your business – but if you're fully briefed, you can be prepared for any challenging questions that come your way.

### 'Who will the interviewer be?'

This will give you a chance to research them and their interviewing style, which can be helpful for your preparation. A word of caution though: the fast-paced nature of the media means things can change, without warning, so be prepared for anything.

### 'Who will I be on with?'

Radio and TV aims to entertain as well as inform. Essentially it's showbiz. So it's common practice, even on the most serious news programmes, for producers to line up interviewees with opposing views. Knowing in advance that you'll be up against your arch-enemy, for example, can help you prepare.

### 'What's coming before and after me?'

Knowing if there's a set-up piece (a pre-prepared feature or segment) can help you get a feel for how a producer intends to cover a story. To go back to the example of the private tutoring firm, if you know there is going to be a set-up piece featuring heartbroken parents who've spent thousands on tutoring only to see their children fail exam after exam, you'll be prepared for the kind of questions that might come your way. If there is a set-up piece, don't be shy about asking to see or hear it (although do be aware this might be impractical).

*'How long will I be on air for?'*

This will give you an idea of how much material to prepare. Regardless of how long you're on for, having one key point you'd like people to take away from the interview can stop you feeling overwhelmed.

## WHAT TO WEAR FOR TV APPEARANCES

Wear something you feel comfortable in, but if in doubt, go more formal: skirts or smart trousers for women and a shirt and tie for men (you can always take the tie off if you feel too dressed up). Skirts can be better for ladies, as you'll probably need to attach a lapel mic to your clothing (if you've ever tried to thread one up the back of a dress – particularly when you're nervous – you'll know what I mean).

Avoid wearing green in recorded interviews (because images may be projected onto it), busy patterns, anything dangly or reflective, badges, obvious fashion labels or slogans, complex necklines and tinted or highly reflective glasses – basically anything that might distract the viewer from what you're saying. And do accept makeup if you're offered it – even if you don't normally wear it (yes, that includes guys), as it will make you look better on screen.

## DURING THE INTERVIEW

**Avoid jargon and technical language.** When you're giving an interview, it's tempting to speak ultra formally or slip into professional jargon – both of which can alienate your audience. While it can feel like you're giving a presentation or a speech, remember you're actually having a conversation with the interviewer. And your audience is people doing pretty mundane things like having coffee and toast at the kitchen table, driving to work or doing the ironing. So if you want to keep them engaged, you'll need to use simple, everyday language and not assume knowledge on their part.

For example, I was delivering some media training to a business network-ing organisation where one of the participants kept using the word 'infrastructure', which can mean different things to different people in different industries (he meant it in the context of rail, road and air). When he stopped talking about infrastructure and started talking about trains, cars and planes, he immediately became more interesting and relevant.

I've worked with some people who complain this is 'dumbing down' – but this couldn't be further from the truth. Using clear, accessible language will help you get your message across to more people – and that's what you want isn't it?

**Take your time.** When you're feeling nervous, it's tempting to jump in and answer questions too quickly. But when you do this, not only do you run the risk of misinterpreting the question, you're much more likely to stumble over your words or sound out of breath. So always take a few seconds to process the question and don't feel you have to keep talking. It's fine to stop once you've made your point and let the interviewer come in with another question.

**Don't be a robot.** Some media trainers will tell you to prepare just a few key points for radio and TV appearances (most interviews are far shorter than you'd imagine). This is good advice, but do make sure you vary your responses. If you trot out the same answer every time, without adapting your message to suit the new question, you'll come across as dull. You might also sound like you're hiding something.

**Be visual – even for radio.** I'm a regular newspaper reviewer on BBC Radio Kent. Just before Christmas, I was invited to taste some non-alcoholic cocktails being made live on the show. Aside from clinking a bit of ice in a glass (and the presenter describing what the bartender was doing) it wasn't easy to convey to listeners what was going on in the studio. But when the presenter tried the cocktail, the bartender said to him 'I can see by the look on your face that you really enjoyed that' – which instantly made it visual.

The moral of this story is: 'show, don't tell'. Instead of telling people about your project or initiative, show them through lively, visual examples and you're far more likely to keep your audience engaged.

**Acknowledge difficult questions...but move things on quickly.** Politicians do this all the time. They acknowledge the question, saying something like 'well that's a really interesting point' or 'Yes I have heard that said' before moving the conversation on using a 'bridging' phrase like 'but what I'm really here to talk about it is...' or 'but I think the issue we really need to address is...'

It's important to use words and phrases that feel comfortable to you though – you don't want to sound like a media-trained robot. Which leads me onto my next point...

**Be yourself.** Remember that radio and TV producers love characters and drama. In fact, some talk about 'casting' rather than booking interviewees for a show. So don't be afraid to show your personality, smile, laugh or make a joke, where appropriate. And resist the temptation to tone down your accent, personality or anything else that makes you uniquely you.

But unless you're invited to – or it is relevant to the discussion – don't try to promote your books, products or services (known in the trade as 'beasting'). You may end up sounding pushy and overpowering.

## HOW TO BECOME A 'GO TO' PERSON FOR MEDIA INTERVIEWS

Securing a few radio and TV interviews is one thing, but if you're serious about using PR to build your influence and authority, you need to be the 'go-to' expert in radio and TV producers' contacts book. Here's some tips on doing just that:

**Be accessible.** Many radio and TV programmes aren't 9-5 outfits, so if you're keen to secure more media appearances, make sure you're contact-able via mobile phone during evenings and weekends. If you're invited into a studio for an interview, do take the opportunity if you can, as this can be a great way to make contacts and connections. If you can't get into the studio, here's a tip for you: producers love experts who have an ISDN line in their office or at home, as you get studio quality sound.

**Be proactive.** Don't sit around waiting for the phone to ring. Find out the names of the producers on the programmes you'd like to contribute to, and give them a call or drop them a line to introduce yourself. Just avoid phoning at obviously busy times (for example, on the hour or half hour on a news programme). And don't be afraid to suggest your own ideas too. I know I've said this in previous chapters, but it's particularly important for radio and TV: make sure your website, social media profiles (and, in particular, your LinkedIn page) are up-to-date, with examples of you in action, if possible.

**Be realistic:** While it is possible to pick up national radio and TV appearances without any prior experience, you may find it easier to get a foot in the door (and a regular gig, like being a newspaper reviewer) on your local radio and/or TV station. People move around a lot in the media; some of the presenters I've met at my local radio station also freelance for national programmes. So not only is this a great way to get broadcast experience, it can also help you build your network of media contacts.

**Be honest:** If you're not comfortable about doing an interview (if you feel it's a subject you don't know well enough, for example), don't be afraid to say 'no'. While it's tempting to say 'yes' in case you don't get asked again, it's much better to recommend someone you feel will be more suitable than bumble your way through an interview on a topic you don't know well enough.

## OVER TO YOU

Identify a programme you'd like to be featured on, find the producer's contact details and give them a call to find out more about how you might be able to help. Do listen to or watch the programme first though.

# GROW YOUR
## *audience*
# & BUILD TRUST
# THROUGH
# ⫶ GUEST ⫶
# CONTENT

# CHAPTER 15

# WHY GUEST CONTENT SHOULD BE PART
## OF YOUR PR STRATEGY

People are often pretty impressed to hear I write for national newspapers, and make regular appearances on radio or TV. They're not so starstruck, however, when they hear I've written a guest blog or been interviewed on a podcast. Yet some of these guest appearances have sent more web traffic – and more importantly, business – my way than traditional media coverage. Which is why I'd strongly urge you to include 'guest content' in your PR strategy.

## WHAT IS 'GUEST CONTENT' AND WHY DOES IT MATTER?

The term 'guest content' generally refers to anything (e.g. blog posts, podcast interviews, videos) you create that is published on someone else's website or platform.

If you don't have much experience of promoting yourself in this way, you may be wondering how creating content for someone else's site can help your business or brand.

But creating guest content not only gets you in front of new audiences (including bigger and more established ones than your own), it can also help you build relationships with influencers and drive traffic to your website.

## HOW DOES 'GUEST CONTENT' DIFFER FROM MAINSTREAM MEDIA COVERAGE?

As I explained in Chapter 3, there are five main types of media content: social media, single author blogs/podcasts, multi author blogs, large media sites and traditional media.

When it comes to creating guest content, you'll generally be focusing on **single author blogs/podcasts** and **multi-author blogs** and while I'd suggest you take a similar approach to pitching as you would with the mainstream media, there are a few differences.

In this chapter, I'll take you through the main things you need to consider when pitching guest content to a podcast host or blogger. I've also included some tips on another type of content – speaking.

## HOW TO PITCH YOURSELF AS A PODCAST GUEST (AND WHY YOU SHOULD BE DOING IT)

A few figures for you:

- Podcast listening grew 23% between 2015 and 2016

- Around 21% of Americans (aged 12 and upwards) have listened to a podcast in the last month – about the same as were active on Twitter

- Weekly podcast listeners consume five shows a week on average

So if you want to promote your business or brand, you need to think beyond traditional PR. You should also be pitching yourself as a podcast guest on shows that are popular with the kind of people you want to reach.

The powerful thing about podcast interviews is that they allow you to get much closer to your prospective audience – quite literally. When people are driving to work, running or cooking the dinner with your voice in their earbuds, you can make a much closer connection and build trust far more quickly.

But most podcast hosts – particularly on popular shows – get dozens of pitches each week. So how do you write a pitch that stands out? Here's how:

# FOCUS ON HOW YOU CAN HELP THE PODCAST HOST (NOT YOURSELF)

As a podcast host, this is what I'm looking for in a guest (I think I'm pretty typical):

1. Someone who can provide great content for my audience. In my case, this is practical 'how to' advice listeners can apply in their business on PR, social media and/or marketing. On another podcast, great content might simply be entertainment or providing information about a specific topic.

2. Someone who has an established online presence in the form of a blog, vlog, podcast and/or has written a book. Not only does these mean they have an audience they can share our podcast interview with (which is good 'PR' for me), it also means I can serve my listeners by directing them towards more useful content.

Sadly, most of the pitches I get are focused on what the person doing the pitching hopes to get out of the interview rather than how they can help my audience.

In many cases, it's clear they haven't even listened to the show (or even scrolled through previous episode titles) to get a feel for the kind of content I offer. In one memorable example, the 'pitcher' was offering an interview with her CEO on the topic of whether you need an MBA to work in the tech industry (I mean, you don't need an MBA to work out that's probably not a good fit for the Soulful PR podcast, do you?).

## LABEL THE SUBJECT HEADER OF YOUR EMAIL

Most podcast hosts and bloggers are actively looking for great content, so label the subject line of your email and they're far more likely to pay attention e.g. *'Podcast interview pitch: How to get big media coverage on a small business budget'*.

## USE THE SUBJECT HEADER TO 'SELL' YOUR IDEA

A concise subject header that summarises your story (ideally in 10 words or less) is far more likely to get a podcast host's attention. As with pitching journalists, resist the temptation to use puns or clever wordplay though; an obscure headline that doesn't mean anything may get ignored.

I've pitched (and successfully placed) lots of podcast interviews on how to do your own PR. While it's tempting to put something like 'how to hit the head-lines' or 'making the news' in the subject header, I know this may mean nothing to a busy podcast host. The more specific I can be, the better.

## KEEP YOUR INTRODUCTION BRIEF

If you're pitching 'cold' it's a good idea to make an introduction (a slightly different approach than when you're pitching to journalists) but keep it brief – otherwise you may lose the podcast host's attention before you've even got started.

e.g. *A quick bit of background – I use my 15 years' experience as a journalist and editor (for the Guardian mainly) to help businesses and brands get media coverage in place like the Huffington Post, Daily Mail, BBC, Entrepreneur and more. I also have a PR blog and podcast.*

## SHOW YOU'VE ACTUALLY LISTENED TO THE PODCAST OR READ THE BLOG

Most of the podcast interview pitches I get are from people who either haven't listened to my podcast and/or haven't given any thought to the kind of content I generally run. Say something that shows you've taken the time and trouble to actually listen to the podcast, and you'll stand out immediately.

E.g. *'I've been following your podcast for a while, and really enjoyed your recent interview with Holly James on how to use Periscope to build influence (been trying out some of Holly's strategies this week – they're fab) and wondered if you might be interested in having me on your show to talk about how to get big media coverage on a small business budget.'*

## SHOW YOU CAN ADD VALUE FOR THEIR AUDIENCE

Most of the podcast pitches I get are quite vague and say things like 'We could chat about branding' or 'we could chat about productivity'. The more specific you can be about the content you could cover – and if it's a business podcast – the practical takeaways for listeners, the better your chances of getting a 'yes.'

*E.g. Here's what I could cover*

- *What kind of stories journalists are looking for (and what they're not)*

- *How to put together a press release or 'pitch' for a newspaper, magazine or radio/TV show*

- *How to find journalists' contact details and how to build relationships with them on social media*

- *How to stay positive when you're hearing the word 'no' more than 'yes' from journalists (which can happen a lot when you're just getting started)*

- *Loads of examples/case studies of authors who've got great press cover-age(both in the UK and overseas, including the US)*

## SHOW HOW YOU CAN HELP THEM GROW THEIR AUDIENCE

If you want to increase your chances of getting a 'yes' from a podcast host, you need to show how you can help them grow their audience by promoting the content to yours. So do include any relevant stats, like the size of your email list and numbers of social media followers.

Don't let not having a big email list or social media following put you off; personally I'd rather get in front of 500 people who are exactly the kind of people I love to work with than 50,000 people who 'sort of' fit. So if you target the right kind of content at the right kind of people, you can usually make a strong case – as long as you're focused on how you can help the podcast host rather than yourself.

*e.g. I have more than 11,000 followers on Twitter and an email list of 5.5k so I'd be able to spread the word about the podcast – and your business – to a decent-sized audience.*

If you're just starting out and your email list is small (or non-existent), focus on the value of the content you can offer.

## SHOW THAT OTHER PEOPLE VALUE YOUR CONTENT

If you've contributed guest content elsewhere, do mention it in your pitch. Seeing that others value your content – particularly if they're well-established podcasters – provides reassurance that you know what you're talking about.

*e.g. 'I've also been interviewed for some other popular podcasts, including Chris Ducker's Youpreneur podcast and Natalie Sisson's Suitcase Entreprener podcast.'*

## MAKE IT AS EASY AS POSSIBLE FOR THE PODCAST HOST TO SAY 'YES'

For most podcast hosts, the interview is the enjoyable bit. Chasing people up for photos, biogs and social media handles can be a pain. So make it as easy for them as possible by providing all of that info in your pitch

E.g. *I really hope you'll be interested in having me as a guest. In the event that you are, here's a few things to (hopefully) make things easier for you.*

1. *A biog (below)*

2. *A photo (attached)*

3. *A link to my calendar so you can book in a time for us to speak*

*Janet Murray helps people get press coverage in newspapers, magazines and on radio and TV. She has 15 years' experience writing and editing for national newspapers and magazines. You can find her PR blog at: www.janetmurray.co.uk.*

*Where you can find Janet:*

- *Website*
- *Twitter*
- *Instagram*

# DON'T FORGET TO FOLLOW-UP

Getting half an hour or longer on a call with someone you admire – or would love to work with in the future – is a great opportunity to start building a business relationship.

So when your interview goes live, don't forget to email the host to thank them for the interview...and get out there and promote it. Email your list, share it on all your social media networks and keep on doing it (I'm still sharing podcast interviews I did a year ago or more on social media).

Remember you haven't just given a podcast interview – you've created a piece of evergreen content together – which is hugely valuable.

# PITCHING GUEST BLOG CONTENT

If you're pitching a guest blog post, you can follow exactly the same guidelines. The only thing I'd add is that, before you send your pitch, it's a good idea to check if (a) the site owner accepts guest contributions (b) they prefer a pitch in the first instance or prefer contributors to send a completed article. Many single and multi-author sites have a page on their website for prospective contributors, which explains exactly what they're looking for and how to get in touch, but if in doubt, email the site owner and ask. And when it comes to tracking down their email address, you can use exactly the same tactics you'd use to find journalists' contact details (those I shared in Chapter 8).

# HOW TO FIND GUEST CONTENT OPPORTUNITIES

A quick search in itunes or Stitcher, in the categories that relate to your expertise, should throw up plenty of podcasts you could, potentially, be a guest on. A Google search, using keywords that relate to your expertise may also be fruitful, as might joining relevant online communities. For example, once a week, members of the She Podcasts Facebook group are invited to put a call out for guests or put themselves forward to appear on others' shows. I also trawl sites like Forbes, Business Insider and Entrepreneur for round-up posts on popular business podcasts.

As with any aspect of your PR, it's important to be strategic. You may be mad about a particular blog or podcast, but if the people you want to reach aren't, you could be wasting your time. And I can't emphasise enough how important it is for you to listen before you pitch; not only is it polite to the podcast host, it could also save you time pitching to a show that might not get you in front of the people you want to reach.

# A WORD ABOUT PITCHING YOURSELF AS A SPEAKER

Speaking at live conferences, workshops and on online summits or webinars can be another great way to promote your brand and get in front of new audiences. There are two ways you can pitch yourself as a speaker: send an email pitch (the guidelines I set out for pitching yourself as a podcast guest work well for pitching speaking opportunities) or respond to a 'call for speakers'. As with any pitch you make, the more you focus on the value you can add (rather than what you can gain from the experience) the better chance you'll have of getting a 'yes'.

Organisers of big events generally send out a 'call for speakers' as much as a year in advance (sometimes even more). The application process usually involves filling out an online application form outlining any relevant experience. You may even be asked to submit a show reel or video of you speaking.

This presents a 'chicken and egg' situation; if you don't have much experience, you might struggle to get hired as a speaker (particularly if there's a fee involved). Giving talks at local schools, community groups or local business networking events can be a great way to get started, as can joining a speakers' organisation like Toastmasters, where you can practise your craft.

When it comes to online speaking opportunities, if you host your own webinars or summits, you're in a far stronger position to pitch yourself as a guest on other peoples' – so why not just get started?

One of the biggest mistakes I see people making in pitches for speaking opportunities is not being specific enough about what they can talk about. Having two or three 'talks' can save you time and hassle. I currently have three:

- *How to get big media coverage on a small business budget*

- *Your press release is breaking my heart (a totally unconventional guide to selling your story in the media)* (yep, the title of this book!)

- *How to build relationships with journalists online (without being a crazy stalker)*

This doesn't mean every speaking pitch should be identical (you can even change the title), it just gives you a framework to work to and means you don't have to reinvent the wheel for every speaking proposal.

## HOW TO FIND SPEAKING OPPORTUNITIES

If you're new to speaking, starting local can be a good idea. Business networking groups can be a good place to start, as most are looking for experts to speak at their events.

If you've already got some experience under your belt, a Google search using the phrase "call for speakers" (along with keywords relating to your preferred topics and location) should also throw up some opportunities. Creating a Google alert with the phrase and keywords that relate to your preferred location and/or area of expertise should help you find out about speaking opportunities as soon as the call for speakers goes out.

The website Lanyrd has a huge database of events all around the world and allows you to track events and create a profile with your information for event organisers to find you.

Another tip is to add 'public speaker' to your LinkedIn profile (along with your showreel and/or testimonials from organisers of events you've spoken at) as many event organisers search there for speakers.

Joining networking groups and relevant online communities can help a lot. For example, I belong to the Women Who Speak Facebook group where members will often share speaking opportunities they've heard about that don't necessarily relate to their area of expertise.

You might also want to look into TEDx. This is an international community that organizes TED-style events (TED is a nonprofit devoted to spreading ideas in the form of short, powerful talks). TEDx events are produced independently of TED conferences and each event curates speakers on their own, based on TED's format and rules. The application process is tough, but giving a TEDx talk carries a lot of kudos and, as the event is recorded, will provided you with a 'showreel' you can share with event organisers.

## OVER TO YOU

If you want to use guest content to grow your authority, developing a daily pitching habit can help you make it happen. I pitch something – to the traditional media, a large news site or a podcast – every single day. Give or take a few days for holidays, sickness and exceptionally busy periods, and that's over 300 pitches a year. They don't all work out, but many of them do which is why I've created so much guest content. Are you willing to devote ten minutes a day to doing something that could make a huge difference to your business? Tweet me at #dailypitch to let me know you're in and let's keep each other accountable.

## USEFUL LINKS

Lanyrd
*www.lanyrd.com*

Toastmasters
*www.toastmasters.org*

TEDx
*tedxtalks.ted.com*

❦

*When*

# HATERS
# HATE
## IT'S NOT ABOUT
☞ YOU

# ⇛ CHAPTER 16 ⇚

# HATERS GONNA HATE
## DEALING WITH BEING IN THE MEDIA SPOTLIGHT

A few years back, a former TV producer turned writer called Samantha Brick wrote an article entitled 'Why women hate me for being beautiful' in the Daily Mail, which whipped up a mighty media storm in the UK.

Many of the leading magazine and newspaper columnists wrote about it, all the popular TV shows were covering it and everyone was talking about it on social media. The general consensus was this: how could a woman who was pleasant looking, but arguably not catwalk material, have the audacity to claim she was beautiful. 'Career suicide' and 'a laughing stock' were typical of the insults being traded about her.

Was this career suicide for Samantha Brick? Was it heck. She's gone on to write dozens more articles for the Daily Mail (and elsewhere), get a publishing deal and write a book about her experience of running away to France to marry her French lover (which is a great read, by the way).

I share this because it's a reminder to keep things in perspective. A journalist spelling your name incorrectly or writing something that doesn't paint your business in the glowing light you were hoping for is not a crisis. Neither are negative online comments or columnists/bloggers writing critical follow-ups to articles you've been featured in (believe me, I've been there).

Media coverage that suggests your products or services are harmful to people – or brings your personal reputation into question – could be. But with sensitive handling, you can minimise the damage.

With that in mind, here are some tips on handling life in the media spotlight.

## BE PREPARED FOR CRITICISM

If you're going to put yourself in the media spotlight, people are going to criticise you. There will be people out there who love what you do. But there will be others who don't and some of them will tell you *exactly* what they think. On Twitter. On your Facebook page. Or – if you're really lucky – they might even send you a lengthy email explaining, point-by-point, exactly why you suck. .

These kind of people are generally in the minority, but their criticism can knock your confidence – and give you temporary amnesia over the dozens of people who've said *nice* things about what you do.

In my 15 years as a journalist and editor, I've had my fair share of haters: from the person who posted online that he'd used my article in a writing class (as an example of how *not t*o write) to the guy who tweeted to observe 'how someone so ugly [me] could have such a beautiful daughter' to the guy who left the following Facebook message: "So you had a miscarriage. So what? What makes you think people want to read about it in a newspaper?' Ouch.

## WHY YOU SHOULD FEED YOUR HATERS

Unless it's personally insulting – or just plain silly (like the person who said I had terrible taste in furniture, having seen my house in a press photograph), I try to reply to every comment.

The way I see it, if someone has taken the time to post a comment, I owe them the courtesy of a reply – an approach that seems to command grudging respect from even the most mean-spirited person.

I'm not saying this is the right strategy for everyone – I know some people who cope simply by not reading the comments at all – but it certainly worth considering. After all, if you're stonewalling your critics, what does that say about your brand?

## DON'T TAKE THINGS PERSONALLY

Always remember that when haters hate, it's not about you. It's down to their own life experiences, opinions and how they see the world – which is why there's no point taking things personally.

That's not to say you shouldn't ask yourself if there's any truth in what people are saying. While their approach might seem spiteful, there is always something to learn from the experience.

Perhaps you did make a mistake or maybe there is something you can improve about what you do. Acknowledging this can often be enough to disarm your haters.

## HANDLING MISTAKES

If a journalist makes a mistake or publishes something you're not happy with, don't lose your cool. Most media outlets have robust systems for dealing with corrections and clarifications, so just ask to speak to the person who deals with that and explain the situation. You'll probably be pleasantly surprised how quickly and efficiently your complaint is dealt with.

Do be aware, however, of the difference between a mistake (which can and should be corrected) and you being unhappy with how the story has been reported. For example, I recently heard a story about a hotel owner who – despite getting a five star review from a classy weekend newspaper supplement – was making a fuss because his duty manager wasn't mentioned in the piece. Remember, a journalist is under no obligation to include information you think is important – it's their job to report the story in a fair and balanced way. And they are definitely not obliged to show you their article before it is published (in fact it would be unethical for them to do so).

The only exception to this is a first-person article; if it is meant to be your words, the journalist should really show you the final version – complete with any cuts or edits – before it is published.

## DEALING WITH A GENUINE MEDIA CRISIS

If you find yourself in the midst of a genuine media crisis – for example, someone has been harmed by your product or service – the worst thing you can do is say nothing or 'no comment.'

If you ignore journalists, it may appear as if you have something to hide. It may also look like you don't care about your customers, which is probably the most long-term damage you can do to your business.

That's not to say you need to respond immediately, or give an interview to every journalist that calls. As with any crisis, it's vital to identify the problem and establish the facts first. Once you've prepared a response – that shows you recognise the seriousness of the situation and are doing something about it – get it up on your website and/or on your social media networks. You may then decide to give interviews to key journalists.

Update your social networks as soon as information becomes available and respond calmly to every comment if you can – even if it's negative. Turn off scheduled social media updates and concentrate your efforts on keeping people updated. If it's really serious, you might want to create a dedicated page on your website you can direct people to which contains your most up-to-date news.

## KEEP YOUR SENSE OF HUMOUR

When you're in the middle of a crisis or 'hater storm' you may feel like crawling into bed and lying there with the covers over your head until it's all over. This is perfectly natural. Remind yourself that everything passes and that people will soon get bored and move onto the next thing (or person). Talking to family and friends who can help you keep things in perspective – and help you see the funny side of things – can help too.

And do bear in mind that most media storms die down as quickly as they blow up. In a 24/7 news culture when there's always something for people to feel outraged about it – people quickly get bored and move onto the next thing.

## OVER TO YOU

Preparing for a media crisis starts before the crisis has actually happened, so set aside some time to create a strategy. This doesn't need to be anything grand – a one sider outlining the potential risks and how you'd respond is enough. Head over to www.janetmurray.co.uk/books to get your free media crisis strategy template.

A GOOD
**PR PRO**
*will tell you*

WHEN YOU'RE
**WRONG**

# ⥤ CHAPTER 17 ⥢

# HIRING A DECENT PR PRO

I f you've read this far, I'm hoping I've convinced you that you can and should be hands-on with your PR. But I also know that handling your own PR may not be practical; you're a busy person and there are only so many hours in the day, so there may come a time when you need to outsource. In this chapter, I'll take you through everything you need to consider to find the right person or team for the job.

## DO YOU REALLY NEED TO OUTSOURCE?

The first question to ask yourself is: 'what do I actually need help with?' It may sound obvious, but if you don't give it some thought, you could end up outsourcing unnecessarily.

It could be, for example, that you're happy to develop story ideas and do the pitching yourself, but need help researching target publications or finding journalists' contact details (both tasks that can easily be outsourced to a virtual assistant) or writing press releases (which can be outsourced to a freelance writer).

Which leads me to the next question: do you have the resources to do this in your existing team?' I've worked with several small businesses who initially said they wanted to outsource their PR, but after talking things through, it quickly became clear they already had the right people in the team – they just didn't have the relevant experience.

Remember that no PR company or consultant will know your business like your current team does. Investing in upskilling someone you're already working with – a virtual assistant with good research and/or copywriting skills, for example – could save you time and money.

## HOW TO FIND A GREAT PR PRO

If you've asked yourself these questions and still feel you need to outsource, start by asking for personal recommendations. You can also try LinkedIn or a good old-fashioned Google search for PR experts in your area (and I'd generally recommend someone local, as they should already have connections with your local press).

I'd definitely recommend a freelancer or small company over a big agency. While no PR consultant will ever know or love your business like you do, a smaller outfit, with fewer clients can usually offer more personal attention. I've also heard far too many horror stories about big agencies who get their most experienced PR pros to pitch for the contract, then put juniors on the day-to-day work. The result? Little or no press coverage.

## CHECKING OUT THE CREDENTIALS OF POTENTIAL HIRES

I'm not going to beat about the bush: sadly there are people out there, who will take your money for writing pointless press releases and articles that never get picked up by the press. So do your research on prospective hires.

Personally, I wouldn't be too fussed about PR qualifications (a background in journalism is probably more useful); what really matters is results. So I'd definitely ask to see examples of press coverage they've got for clients and testimonials (and don't be afraid to contact the people who wrote those testimonials for further information).

I'd also spend some time seeing how they operate on social media. Are they interacting with journalists on Twitter or LinkedIn? Are they using hashtags like #journorequest to respond to journalists requests on behalf of their clients? Are they using social media to promote their business (not by 'broadcasting' their own news, but by sharing content prospective clients might find useful)?

Look also at how they promote their own business. Do they write for the Huffington Post and/or get published regularly in the national press themselves? Have they got a blog where they share PR advice and/or write guest posts on the topic? Is their LinkedIn profile fully completed with a catchy headline, testimonials and digital downloads or video?

What you really need is someone who walks the talk; after all, if they're not promoting their own business effectively, how can you be sure they'll be any good at doing your PR?

## SPOTTING THE DANGER SIGNS

Don't be afraid to ask prospective hires how they might approach a specific challenge e.g. a product launch or event you've got coming up. And if they start talking about writing a press release for you and sending it out to lots of journalists, I hope you now know enough to recognise this as a potential 'red flag'.

Beware also of PR companies or consultants who make guarantees about how much press coverage they can get you. As I'm sure you're now aware, there are no guarantees in PR. This is because you can't control the news agenda – nobody can.

So you can work your socks off on a pitch or PR campaign, but if something more newsworthy comes along e.g. a terrorist attack or the sudden death of a celebrity on the day your story is due to run, it may well get spiked. In fact your story could get binned in favour of something far less dramatic.

Finally, look for someone who is prepared to tell you when you're wrong. I heard a PR consultant say recently that her job was about 'balancing the needs of her client and journalists.' This is rubbish. If you've taken one thing away from this book, I hope it's that – like it or not – getting press coverage is about what journalists want, not you.

A PR consultant who will send out a press release or pitch just because you've told them to (rather than because they think journalists will be interested) is actually acting against your best interests. If you get a reputation for sending out irrelevant press releases and story ideas, journalists will start to recognise your business name – for all the wrong reasons. So 'can you tell me about a time you disagreed with a client?' can be a really great question to ask when you're checking out potential hires.

A personal tip from me: people who've done PR for charities are usually excellent. They're resourceful, well-informed and understand what makes a media story (in my experience, anyway).

## WORKING WITH A PR CONSULTANT OR AGENCY

If you hired a plumber to fix your toilet or an architect to design an extension for your house, you'd take their professional advice wouldn't you?

So if you've hired a PR consultant or agency – and checked their credentials carefully – then for God's sake...listen to what they have to say.

I hear so many stories of small business owners who hire PR firms and then blatantly disregard their advice. The result? You've guessed it: no press coverage.

I'm not saying you shouldn't ever challenge your PR consultant – you totally should – but value their expertise, and treat them as a professional they are, and you'll get so much more out of the partnership.

And do remember that there is no such thing as 'set and forget' PR. Just because you're paying someone to handle your PR, doesn't mean you can just leave them to it. You need to make yourself available to talk to them on a regular basis and, if they ask you for something (some copy for a pitch or press release, for example) or call you to see if you're free to talk to a journalist, make getting back to them a priority. As you've probably gathered from reading this book, journalists move quickly; if you don't make the deadline – or can't make yourself available for an interview – there are no second chances. They'll simply find someone else to talk to.

# ⋛OVER AND OUT⋚

**S**o we've come to the end of our journey together. If you take one thing away from this book I hope it's this: PR is simply about telling stories.

Master the art of telling the right stories to the right people at the right time, and you'll have no trouble getting media coverage for your business or brand.

I'm not saying it will be easy; you'll get countless rejections and let downs. Some journalists will keep you dangling for months before they respond to your pitch or publish your work. You may get so frustrated, you feel like giving up.

But when you see the impact consistent, high-profile media coverage can have on your business or brand, I promise it will be worthwhile.

They key word here is 'consistent'. I've lost count of the number of people who've told me that PR doesn't work for them because they had an article in a newspaper once and didn't get any business from it.

Would you expect to get new clients or a stream of speaking invitations from one Tweet or Facebook post? Of course not. To get engagement on social media, you need to show up and take action, every single day – even when no one is listening. Keep showing up, starting conversations and sharing great content and people will start to notice you.

PR is exactly the same.

As I never get tired of saying: if you're persistent, consistent and willing to learn from your mistakes, you will get there in end.

Pinky promise.

And if you find yourself feeling stuck, remember you don't have to do it alone.

My blog (www.janetmurray.co.uk) and podcast (janetmurray.co.uk/category /podcast) are full of practical resources that will help you sell your stories into the media.

You'll also find tremendous support in my Soulful PR Facebook Community (www.facebook.com/groups/SoulfulPRcommunity).

You can also reach out to me on Twitter (@janmurrayuk) or by email (janet@janetmurray.co.uk).

If you want daily support with your PR journey, you may even want to join the Soulful PR Business Club (learn.janetmurray.co.uk/courses/soulful-pr-business - club) my online community for businesses and brands who want to build their influence in the media.

Good Luck!

# ⩨ ABOUT THE AUTHOR ⩨

Janet Murray is a British journalist and PR coach who helps businesses and brands tell their story in the media. She's written for dozens of national newspapers (including the Guardian, Huffington Post, Daily Telegraph, Entrepreneur, Independent, Daily Mail, Sun and more), many consumer titles and made dozens of appearances on radio and TV. She's also a blogger, speaker and podcaster. Janet lives near London with her husband and ten-year-old daughter and runs her business from her garden 'shedquarters', local coffee shop or wherever she happens to be in the world (and thanks her lucky stars for it every day). Find out more about her at: www.janetmurray.co.uk.

# ≑ ACKNOWLEDGEMENTS ≑

Ed Miller

Sarah Newton

Nikki Armytage

Jo Francis

Lisa Crossland

Tracey Tester

Alexia Leachman

Angela Henderson

Ania Krasniewska

Caroline McCullough

Danny Lynch

Elizabeth McCourt

Genevieve Brading

Harriet Minter

Jennifer D Begg

Jessica Friend

Julia Shervington

Karen Lisa Laing

Katy Pollard

Kelly Exeter

Laure Moyle

Laurens Bonnema

Mark Ferguson

Melanie Haynes

Phil Pallen

Rob Lawrence

Sue Allison

Timothy Lewis

Printed in Great Britain
by Amazon